CALIFORNIA
FRUIT & VEGETABLE GARDENING

First published in 2012 by Cool Springs Press, an imprint of the Quayside Publishing Group, 400 First Avenue North, Suite 300, Minneapolis, MN 55401 USA.

Cool Springs Press titles are also available at discounts in bulk quantity for industrial or sales-promotional use. For details write to Special Sales Manager at Cool Springs Press, 400 First Avenue North, Suite 300, Minneapolis, MN 55401 USA.

To find out more about our books, visit us online at www.coolspringspress.com.

ISBN-13: 978-1-59186-528-5

Library of Congress Cataloging-in-Publication Data

Splan, Claire.
    California fruit & vegetable gardening : plant, grow, and eat the best edibles for California gardens / Claire Splan.
        p. cm.
    Includes index.
    ISBN 978-1-59186-528-5 (pbk.)
    1. Fruit--California. 2. Vegetables--Californias. 3. Herbs--California. 4. Nuts--California. 5. Gardening--California. I. Title. II. Title: California fruit and vegetable gardening. III. Title: Plant, grow, and eat the best edibles for California gardens.

    SB355.5.C2S65 2012
    634.09794--dc23

                                                    2011039002

President/CEO: Ken Fund
Group Publisher: Bryan Trandem
Publisher: Ray Wolf
Senior Editor: Billie Brownell
Editor: Kathy Franz
Creative Director: Michele Lanci
Design Manager: Kim Winscher
Production Manager: Hollie Kilroy
Photo Researcher: Bryan Stusse
Production: S.E. Anderson

Printed in China

10 9 8 7 6 5 4 3 2 1

CALIFORNIA
FRUIT & VEGETABLE GARDENING

CLAIRE SPLAN

COOL
SPRINGS
PRESS

Growing Successful Gardeners™

MINNEAPOLIS, MINNESOTA

CONTENTS

DEDICATION 6

ACKNOWLEDGMENTS 7

WHERE IN CALIFORNIA ARE YOU?
THE USDA HARDINESS ZONE MAP 8

GARDENING IN CALIFORNIA 11

GROWING YOUR OWN: THE GARDEN 15

- *How to Get Started* 16
- *Starting at the Beginning with Seeds* 34
- *Creating the Perfect Soil* 42
- *Watering & Other Necessities* 50

PESTS & DISEASES 61

- *Bugs* 62
- *Diseases* 76

FRUITS, HERBS, NUTS & VEGETABLES 87

Almond	Corn	Peach
Apple	Cucumber	Pear
Apricot	Eggplant	Pecan
Artichoke	Fig	Pepper
Asparagus	Garlic	Persimmon
Avocado	Grape	Pineapple guava
Banana	Guava	Plum
Basil	Kale	Pomegranate
Bean	Kiwi	Potato
Beet	Kohlrabi	Quince
Blueberry	Leek	Radish
Brambleberry	Lettuce	Rhubarb
Broccoli	Loquat	Spinach
Brussels sprouts	Melon	Squash
Cabbage	Okra	Strawberry
Carrot	Olive	Sweet potato
Cauliflower	Onion	Swiss chard
Celery	Parsley	Thyme
Cherry	Parsnip	Tomato
Cilantro	Passion fruit	Turnip
Citrus	Peas	

GLOSSARY   226

RESOURCES   233

FOR FURTHER READING   235

PHOTOGRAPHY CREDITS   237

GARDEN NOTES   238

INDEX   248

MEET CLAIRE SPLAN   255

DEDICATION

For my mother, Beverly Splan, who taught me the importance of playing in the dirt.

ACKNOWLEDGMENTS

Writing this book was one of the biggest challenges I've ever attempted and one I'm certain I could not have faced alone. I know very well that there are unseen contributors to any book that is ever produced, and this book is no different. I'd like to thank Billie Brownell and Kathy Franz at Cool Springs Press for their considerable guidance in getting this book written. Thanks also to Chris McLaughlin, who performed the unenviable task of making sure this book reflects the reality of California gardening—the good, the bad, and the ugly. Thank you to Tracy Stanley and Michele Lanci at Quayside, as well as countless other individuals who contributed to the making of this book. And to Katie Elzer-Peters, who passed my name on to the folks at Cool Springs Press, a very big thank-you.

And to my family and friends who have long supported my dream of writing a book: You've been very patient! Thanks!

WHERE IN CALIFORNIA ARE YOU? THE USDA HARDINESS ZONE MAP

Cold-hardiness zone designations were developed by the United States Department of Agriculture (USDA) to indicate the minimum average temperature for that region. A zone assigned to a plant indicates the lowest temperature at which the plant can normally be expected to survive. California has zones ranging from 4b (the coldest) to 11. Though a plant may grow in zones outside its recommended zone range, the zone ratings are a good indication of which plants to consider for your landscape.

California is a big place with many different climates. Before you start planning your garden, take a look at the map here and identify your USDA hardiness zone. This magic number will be an important aid in your plant selection. You'll find much more information about the USDA zones, as well as other zoning systems, in the section "What's Your Number? Zones and Chill Hours" starting on page 26.

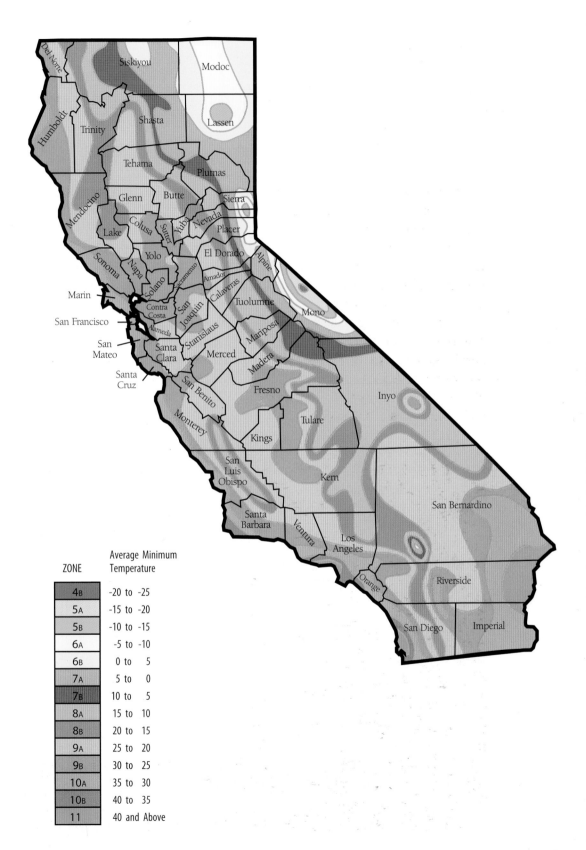

ZONE	Average Minimum Temperature
4B	-20 to -25
5A	-15 to -20
5B	-10 to -15
6A	-5 to -10
6B	0 to 5
7A	5 to 0
7B	10 to 5
8A	15 to 10
8B	20 to 15
9A	25 to 20
9B	30 to 25
10A	35 to 30
10B	40 to 35
11	40 and Above

GARDENING IN CALIFORNIA

We've all seen the commercials, and we know the stereotypes about California: blue skies; endless sunshine; orange groves; rolling vineyards; everything healthy, lush, and green. And it's mostly true—well, up to a point.

The reality is that while gardening in California is in many ways a remarkably easy endeavor, it is in other ways quite challenging. The same temperate climate that can make for blessedly long growing seasons can also give garden pests an environment in which to thrive without the killing freezes in some parts of the state that keep their populations in check. Fertile soil doesn't just grow good tomatoes; it also grows bad weeds. And that endless sunshine has at times led to drought and water rationing. Add to that the little complication of climate change. Yes, it's real. Yes, it's already happening. And it is changing the way things grow in our gardens.

But I think the biggest challenge that California gardeners face is this: it's all just so tempting! It's so easy to think that *anything* will grow here, that all you have to do is plop a seed or a plant in a hole in the ground and it will reward you with flowers, fruit, veggies, next year's seeds, and maybe a cure for heart disease and cancer too. Not that I'm opposed to any gardener's enthusiasm. I applaud it. I practice it. I depend upon it. And I get tripped up by it often enough to keep me humble and remind me that there is always more to learn and that nature is never finished teaching us who's really in charge here.

When I first considered writing a book about growing edibles *in California*, it occurred to me that it was like trying to write a book about gardening *on planet Earth*. California is not a small place, and it is known for its diverse environment. Unlike most other states, California is a smorgasbord of climates and microclimates. We don't have just a few USDA horticultural zones running through the state, we have fourteen of them. And when you consider Sunset zones (developed by *Sunset* magazine), the number shoots up even higher. Soil types? We've got 'em all, from the sandy coastal areas to the hard clay of the inland areas, with pockets of beautiful loam in between. Soils can be more acidic in the north where rainfall is high and more alkaline in the drier south. My experience gardening in the Bay Area is pretty different from that of someone gardening in the Southern

California desert, or the Sierras, or the Central Valley, or the Northern California coast. In the end, gardening, like politics, is always local.

But somehow, it all works. It must, because California's agriculture industry plays a major part in feeding the world. Food wants to grow here. And from the Native Americans who first farmed here to the hippies who "returned to the land," Californians have always loved to grow food.

We love to eat food too. And that "foodie" culture that emphasizes fresh fruits and vegetables, grown locally and organically whenever possible, is a driving force in Californians' renewed interest in growing fruits and vegetables at home. We may not all be able to cook like Alice Waters, but we can follow her lead by incorporating the freshest possible produce in our daily diets. It doesn't get any fresher than something crisp and juicy picked right from your backyard.

Whether you plan to grow just a few fruits or veggies to supplement what you buy in the store or farmers markets or aim to grow as much of your produce as possible, the methods are pretty much the same. But as I warned earlier, don't succumb to the temptation of growing *everything all at once*. Start with a few crops, then add a few more. Rotate planting spaces to keep the soil healthy, and sow seeds successively to prolong the harvest. Add some fruit trees if you have the space and some perennial vegetables that will provide harvests for several years from that one planting. Think long term and high nutrition, and just keep planting.

Most important, remember that gardening is not a project to be completed; it is a path to follow. Some days, some seasons even, are rocky and rough and less rewarding than you'd hoped, but others are lush and simple and beyond bountiful. Every gardener has an occasional bum crop, and every gardener has an occasional bumper crop. Treat your land with respect, practice sustainable gardening methods, and keep planting. You will be rewarded. And remember the words of another land-loving Californian, Robert Louis Stevenson: "Don't judge each day by the harvest you reap, but by the seeds you plant."

Now, let's get dirty.

GROWING YOUR OWN: THE GARDEN

Is gardening simple? Yes. And no. It's simple enough that children can do it. And it's complicated enough that once you start, you will never stop learning how to do it better. And although an understanding of the science of plants helps, this isn't, as they say, rocket science. Don't think of what follows here as an instruction manual. Think of it more as a tour guide to your own garden and what lives there. Tours aren't complicated, but there may be some unexpected twists and turns, some sights you never thought you'd see, some advice from the locals that ensures a better time. It's time to get on the gardening bus!

HOW TO GET STARTED

Nine Reasons Why You Should Grow Your Own

In a recent early summer garden trends survey, the Garden Writers Association reported that 43% of households in the United States were adding vegetable gardens. Growing edibles is definitely in vogue, but surely there are better reasons to do this than "everybody's doing it." I'll give you nine of them:

1. **You'll redefine what "fresh" means.** Some edibles lose a lot of their nutrients and much of their flavor by the time you purchase them at the supermarket, store them in your refrigerator, and then cook and eat them. In most cases, consuming vegetables as soon as possible after harvest means that you get their peak nutritional value with more flavor than you'd have thought possible.

2. **You'll try something different.** There are varieties of fruits and vegetables available to home gardeners that you will never see on supermarket shelves. Many heirloom varieties can't be commercially grown because they just don't ship or store well. But with a few

packets of seeds, you'll be able to explore a whole world of edibles in colors and flavors you never knew existed.

3. **You'll know what you're eating.** Some store-bought produce has enough contaminants on them to give you nightmares (or worse). When you grow your own fruits and vegetables, you know exactly what's gone into growing them. You can grow them completely organically or at least with a bare minimum of inorganic materials.

4. **You'll save some money.** Seeds, water, maybe some soil amendments. That doesn't add up to much. Garden writer Rosalind Creasy recently grew $750 worth of organic produce in a 100-square-foot garden at a cost of just $65. Granted, she's more experienced at this than most of us, but even a novice gardener can save a lot of money.

5. **You'll be able to avoid the next food scare.** *E. coli* in spinach and sprouts. Salmonella in tomatoes and cilantro. Listeria in cantaloupes. These are some of the recent food safety issues that have affected fresh commercially grown produce. And you can bet there will be more to come. Your garden-grown fruits and vegetables are much less prone to these problems with healthy gardening practices. (And remember, you should cover fruits and veggies in the fridge.)

6. **You'll get a healthy workout.** While you're out in the sunshine gardening, your body will be soaking up much-needed vitamin D, which is essential for bone health and general well-being. You'll also be giving your muscles a workout and burning calories at an average rate of 272 per hour.

7. **You'll feel better with dirt under your fingernails.** There's a bacterium in dirt called *Mycobacterium vaccae* that has been found to increase the production of serotonin and stimulate the immune systems of mice. Scientists are now studying how this bacterium, which is already used as a vaccine for tuberculosis and a treatment for cancer patients and asthma sufferers, may be used to treat mood

disorders. The theory is that the bacterium prompts the body's immune cells to release cytokines, which activate sensory nerves stimulating the brain. The brain responds by activating serotonin neurons, which, again, lift the mood. Scientists further hypothesize that prolonged exposure to *M. vaccae* could benefit us by maintaining healthier immune systems.

8. **You'll teach your children.** School gardens have demonstrated that kids learn broad lessons from gardening—lessons about science and nature, about home economics and self-sufficiency, about nutrition and healthy living. Bringing those lessons home in their own gardens will only make them more real and more valuable. They'll thank you later.

9. **You'll be able to share.** If your gardening efforts are rewarded with a bumper crop, you don't have to worry about how you'll possibly be able to get it all preserved. You can simply pass it on. Thanks to the recent recession, food banks across the country need to feed more people than ever. AmpleHarvest.org will point you toward a food bank near you that will happily take some of that zucchini off your hands.

Getting Started

The first thing to remember when planting a vegetable garden is that you don't have to feed the whole neighborhood. In other words, it's best to start small with just a few crops. And if possible, try to keep your vegetable garden contained to one space. Sometimes that doesn't work and you need to sneak a few vegetables among your flowers or add a container where there's good sun exposure. The benefit of having your edibles all in one area, though, is that you can work on improving the soil in that area before you plant or you can group plants by their water needs. However you arrange your garden, newbie gardeners will probably have greater success if they don't get carried away and plant too much.

One tip you will find helpful down the road is to take notes on what you're doing. You might start a garden journal or a blog or just scribble a few notes on a calendar. Having something to look back on that reminds you when you planted or transplanted, the last time you applied fertilizer, or what varieties you tried and how they turned out will help you make

decisions in the future about what to grow and what you might want to do differently. It doesn't have to be anything fancy or well written, but having one fixed place where you log the important details of your garden will pay off sooner than you might imagine.

And here's another piece of advice: Don't just take my advice. Talk to other gardeners. Talk to the staff at your local nurseries. Call your County Extension office if you have specific questions; they train Master Gardeners who have immense gardening knowledge and are happy to share it. And use the Internet's vast gardening resources when you need to search for information quickly, identify a plant, or buy seeds and plants you can't find locally.

Planning the Garden

Where to Grow?

In California, gardens can be very big or very, very small. Some gardeners will have a number of options for locating their gardens; other gardeners may have to make do with the little bit of land they have. Regardless of how big it will be, every gardener will have to consider basic gardening needs when choosing the location for an edible garden.

Unless you live in the desert, where some plants will require afternoon shade, your garden should be in full sun. "Full sun" means at least eight hours a day of unblocked sunshine. Some of us do horrible jobs of estimating the amount of sun a site gets. If you want to be really accurate, you can buy gadgets from garden supply companies that you stick in the ground for a day, and they will tell you whether the site gets full sun, part sun, part shade, or full shade.

You also want to consider how well the site drains. Almost every plant covered in this book will not thrive in poorly drained soil. To test the drainage, dig a hole 12 inches deep and 12 inches wide and insert a yardstick in it. Fill the hole to the top with water and let it drain completely. Then fill it again, using a watch to time how quickly it drains out. It should drain at a

rate of 1 to 2 inches per hour. If it drains faster or slower, your plants will either be underwatered or waterlogged. Either way, the drainage can be improved by working generous amounts of compost into the soil.

Think about access to water too. Is the site reachable with a hose, or better yet, does it have irrigation already installed? A reliable drip irrigation system can be a gardener's best friend, and if you can put a drip system in, you will be glad you did.

When determining where to plant fruit or nut trees, in addition to all of the above, you need to consider soil depth and root systems. Some trees are shallow-rooted, but others have deep taproots and will only grow where the soil is several feet deep with no rocks to impede their growth. You should also avoid planting some fruit trees close to windows; they may need to be sprayed for insect or disease control, and the sprays can be messy.

Planting fruits and vegetables in your front yard has become a controversial issue in some towns, but it shouldn't be. There's no reason a well-tended vegetable garden can't be pleasant to look at. But before you plant, you may want to check city ordinances or homeowner association bylaws to see if there are any restrictions against growing edibles in the front of your house.

How Big Should You Go?

When it comes to figuring out how big to make your garden, there are a few factors to consider. First, the size of your garden should have everything to do with how much of your garden is in full sun. Use an area that sees less sun for some part-shade herbs. If you have only a small space with really good exposure, start there and see how densely you can reasonably plant. Very often, plants need sun even more than they need room.

Second, think about how much time you have to give to the garden. Don't plant more than you have time to maintain. An untended vegetable garden is a sad sight and a waste of resources.

Third, how much do you want to experiment? If you're interested in growing varieties that you've never tried before, you may want to plan to leave a little extra space. That way, you can still have enough room for your tried-and-true favorites, and if the new crops don't do well or are not to your liking, you still have your old standbys. If the heirloom tomatoes you've never grown before are a bust, at least you can have a bountiful crop of your favorite hybrids. Experimenting with new plants is a fun and noble

thing to do, and allowing a little additional space to do it in is probably a good idea.

So how big a space should you plant? The answer is this: just big enough and no bigger.

What to Grow

Want to know what to grow? Look in your refrigerator. Look in your fruit bowl. Look at the recipes you prepare most often. Grow what your family loves to eat. Make a list of the fruits and vegetables you buy most often and compare it to the fruits and vegetables covered in this book. If you live in a zone where it can be grown and you have the room for it, it's probably worth trying.

That being said, if you are new to growing edibles, or new to gardening entirely, I'd suggest trying just two or three crops at a time. A few easy-to-grow warm-season vegetables, such as tomatoes, zucchini, and beans, can be replaced in the fall with cool-season cabbages, broccoli, and beets. Consider some perennial vegetables, such as artichokes, asparagus, and rhubarb; even the ones that take a couple years to start producing will eventually provide years of harvests. Or maybe you'd like to start with some fruit trees, which don't require such constant attention but still yield a huge amount of food for the space.

You might also take a look at the Environmental Working Group's Dirty Dozen:

- ➤ Apples
- ➤ Celery
- ➤ Strawberries
- ➤ Peaches
- ➤ Spinach
- ➤ Nectarines (imported)
- ➤ Grapes (imported)
- ➤ Sweet bell peppers
- ➤ Potatoes
- ➤ Blueberries (imported)
- ➤ Lettuce
- ➤ Kale/Collard greens

These are the twelve commercially grown foods most contaminated with pesticide residue. Every store-bought item on this list that you replace with your own homegrown, pesticide-free harvest means fewer chemicals and toxins your family is consuming.

Flowers with Flavor

There's more to growing edibles than just fruits, vegetables, herbs, and nuts. Don't forget flowers! Some of the blossoms you already have growing could easily find their way into your lunchtime salad or decorate your favorite dessert. Some edible blossoms, like the flowers from scarlet runner beans, squash, and pineapple guava, are discussed in the fruit and vegetable profiles later in this book. But the following is a list of common flowers you can use to cook with or to safely garnish a dish:

- Bachelor's button/Cornflower (*Centaurea cyanus*)
- Bee balm/Bergamot (*Monarda didyma*)
- Borage (*Borago officinalis*)
- Breadseed poppy (*Papaver somniferum*)
- Calendula (*Calendula officinalis*)
- Carnation/Sweet William (*Dianthus*)
- Chamomile (*Matricaria recutita*)
- Chrysanthemum (*Chrysanthemum*)
- Daisy (*Bellis perennis*)
- Dandelion (*Taraxacum officinale*)
- Daylilies (*Hemerocallis*)
- Hibiscus (*Hibiscus rosa-sinensis*)
- Lavender (*Lavendula*)
- Lilac (*Syringa vulgaris*)
- Marigold (*Tagetes tenuifolia*)
- Nasturtium (*Tropaeolum majus*)
- Pansy (*Viola × wittrockiana*)
- Rose (*Rosa*)
- Scented geranium (*Pelargonium*)
- Sunflower (*Helianthus annuus*)
- Sweet violet (*Viola odorata*)
- Tuberous begonias (*Begonia × tuberosa*)

Some of the flowers can be eaten in their entirety; some only have edible petals. With others, such as the breadseed poppy and the sunflower, it's the seeds that are edible. Roses not only have edible petals, but the rose hips are also used for jellies, teas, or other dishes.

It is important to note that any flowers used in food must not be treated with pesticides. Never eat flowers you find growing on the side of the road—who knows what car emissions and other toxins they may have absorbed? Some people can have allergic reactions, particularly to the pollen of some flowers. Because plants may have some parts that are edible and other parts that are highly poisonous, you should research any flower you use in food to make sure you are using only the edible parts.

What Is an Heirloom Plant?

You've probably heard this term recently in cookbooks, in trendy restaurants, in farmers markets, and in nurseries—but what exactly is an heirloom?

Heirlooms aren't just plants that have been around for a long time, though age is a factor. While not a hard and fast rule, 1951 is considered by many to be a cutoff date for heirlooms. Since 1951, commercial plant breeders have introduced a huge number of hybrids. Before that time, cultivars were more likely to be "found" rather than "bred."

In addition to being older varieties, heirlooms are considered "open-pollinated." This just means that heirloom varieties will grow "true" from seed. In other words, if you plant a seed from an heirloom vegetable, the seed will produce a plant and fruit that is the same as the parent plant. Hybrids, on the other hand, may produce sterile seed or seed that will produce a plant that is unlike the parent.

Flavor is the other factor that tends to be characteristic of heirlooms. While modern commercial varieties have been bred for longer shelf life and appearance, heirlooms were chosen specifically for their superior flavor. They may come in striking colors (consider black tomatoes, white eggplants, and blue potatoes), but the flavor is usually what made these varieties popular before they fell out of favor commercially.

There can be a downside to growing heirlooms. Some plants are susceptible to serious diseases such as fusarium wilt and verticillium wilt. Others are just a bit finicky. Some breeders are now grafting heirloom varieties onto hybridized, disease-resistant rootstocks that enable you to have the beauty and flavor of an heirloom without that risk or the frustration.

For most heirlooms, however, you'll need to grow them from seed. For a good selection of heirloom seeds, check out Baker Creek Heirloom Seeds (www.rareseeds.com) or Seed Savers Exchange (www.seedsavers.org).

Map It Out

As you plan your garden, map it out before you start digging! Grab a pencil, paper, and tape measure. Take the measurements of the space that you plan to plant and sketch out a simple grid marked off by feet. Indicate where north is on the diagram. Take the list of what you want to grow and use it to map out a plan with the proper spacing for all the plants. Consider the mature height of each plant so you can avoid having taller plants shading out shorter ones. The plan doesn't have to be complex or perfect. Odds are, you won't follow it exactly anyway. But creating this visual aid in advance forces you to think through how the garden will look, not just at the beginning, but as the plants grow and mature as well.

If you are technologically inclined to the point where you no longer own pencils and paper, some software tools will map out a garden plan. Several of these require purchasing the software, but Gardener's Supply Company has a free Kitchen Garden Planner that is simple to use. Check it out at www.gardeners.com/on/demandware.store/Sites-Gardeners-Site/default/Page-KGPJS.

What's Your Number? Zones and Chill Hours

The most important number for any gardener to know is his or her zone number. The U.S. Department of Agriculture (USDA) has a map that divides the entire U.S. into hardiness zones based on climatic conditions and average minimum temperatures. When you know your zone, you can find out whether or not a plant will be able to survive in your region.

Earlier in the book, in the section called "Where in California Are You? The USDA Hardiness Zone Map," we included a color-coded map of California's 14 USDA hardiness zones. To view the USDA hardiness zone map for the entire country, go to www.usna.usda.gov/Hardzone/

ushzmap.html. You can click on the link for California to get a more detailed look at the state map and also look up lists of plants and their hardiness zones. To find your zone quickly by entering your zip code, go to www.gardenweb.com/zones/zip.cgi.

The USDA is not the only organization in the zoning business, however. The Arbor Day Foundation has their own hardiness zone map, which they updated in 2006 based on more recent climate data. To find your Arbor Day Foundation zone by entering your zip code, go to www.arborday.org/treeinfo/zonelookup.cfm.

Sunset Publishing Corporation has created a more detailed zone map that can help give you an even clearer picture of what your climate is like and what will grow there. Check out the full zone map at www.plantfinder.sunset.com/sunset/plant-home.jsp and click on your region to see your zone.

Sometimes gardeners can be confused to find two different zones for the same location. The USDA zone is the number referred to most often and is the zoning system generally used by nurseries and seed companies. If you only know one zone number for your garden, make it the USDA zone number. The Arbor Day and Sunset zones can help you gather more information about how certain plants will do in your specific area, when you should expect frosts, and how long your growing season is. Knowing your zone(s) is key to making good gardening choices.

In addition to your zone, there's one other number that can help when selecting which fruit and nut trees to grow: your number of *chill* hours. Chill hours are the number of hours that a tree must spend below 45° F in order to blossom and set fruit. The hours can be cumulative, but it is best if they occur in December and January. The number of chill hours in your location will tell you whether you can grow a 'Fuji' apple (600 hours) or if you should go with a lower-chill variety like 'Anna' (200 hours). To find the number of chill hours in your area, go to the website for the University of California's Fruit & Nut Research and Information Center (www.fruitsandnuts.ucdavis.edu/chillcalc/index1.htm). Click the link for your area to retrieve historical data in your county. This will give you the most accurate data for the cumulative winter chill hours between November 1 and February 29.

Growing More in Less Space

No-Row Gardening

Contrary to what gardening books may lead you to believe, there is no law that says that vegetables *must* be planted in rows. Row planting is a holdover from traditional agriculture where it's necessary to plant in rows so laborers can easily work their way through the fields. In a home garden, however, it doesn't always make sense.

On seed packets and even in the plant profiles in this book, you'll see instructions about spacing plants in rows. While the amount of space between plants is important, feel free to forget about the rows. Some seed packets will suggest *broadcasting* seed. That means sprinkling seeds over a prepared bed rather than dropping the seeds in a row. For plants like carrots, radishes, and some lettuces, this can be a much more space-efficient approach. You'll still need to thin plants to allow the recommended growing space, but by not planting in rows, you will be able to squeeze more plants into the same space. Seedlings can also be transplanted in this no-row manner.

Square Foot Gardening

This technique uses raised beds and a grid pattern to plot out squares that are each intensively planted based on the size of the plant. Mel Bartholomew popularized the method many years ago, and it has become particularly popular with gardeners with small gardens or poor soil. The beds are usually 4 × 4 feet or smaller so all plants are easy to reach and floating row covers can easily be added to extend the growing season or deter pests. Square foot gardening produces higher yields per square foot and allows for more efficient watering.

A possible downside to this method is the cost of materials. Besides the cost of the raised-bed materials, there is the cost of the soil mix.

Bartholomew recommends one-third sphagnum peat moss, one-third vermiculite, and one-third compost. Filling multiple raised beds with this mix can get costly, but the higher yield of produce may make it worth it.

Raised Beds

Traditionally, raised beds are simple wooden frameworks built to contain soil above the ground for planting. Raised beds can be constructed in different ways and in different sizes, but they are typically built from untreated wood or composite material. Other materials used to construct raised beds include stone, straw bales, brick, or concrete blocks. They should be at least 6 to 8 inches deep, or 10 to 12

inches deep if you are planning to grow root vegetables such as carrots or potatoes. If accessibility is an issue for you, raised beds may need to be deeper or elevated on tables.

Raised-bed gardening has a lot of advantages. Soil in raised beds warms sooner than the ground soil does, which means that seeds germinate quicker and plants grow better. Soil conditions can be controlled more easily, and contaminated soil can be avoided completely by building raised beds on top of them. Drainage problems can be avoided with raised beds as well.

As with square foot gardening, however, the cost of materials, particularly if you don't have your own supply of good compost, can add up. Wood raised beds will usually last for several years, and composite-constructed beds will last much longer.

Vertical Gardening

Your gardening space isn't limited by the number of square feet you have available for planting. If your garden is small, you can garden up instead of out.

Start with hanging planters. Tomatoes, strawberries, peppers, and many herbs can do great in hanging pots. Take advantage of some new planter designs that can cover an entire wall with planting pockets that you can fill with herbs and other edibles. Try stacking containers, starting with a large

oak barrel at the bottom and increasingly smaller pots on top, with different plants growing in each container. You can also grow vining plants such as cucumbers and melons up trellises to take up less ground space, with the added benefit of keeping the fruit off the ground.

Even trees don't have to take up a lot of space if you think vertically rather than horizontally. Plant fruit trees that can be espaliered flat against a fence or that is a tall, skinny columnar variety. They will produce a surprising amount of fruit in a very small space.

If you have a limited amount of gardening space in full sun, vertical gardening is definitely the way to make the most of that space.

Interplanting

One way to make the most of limited gardening space is to place faster-growing plants in between slower-growing ones. For example, you can plant lettuce seeds surrounding your tomato plants. The lettuces will have matured and been harvested long before the tomato plants are big enough to crowd them out. Another type of interplanting involves mixed plantings of edibles and ornamentals. Not only do they get along fine, but they can be advantageous for each other. Flowers can attract more pollinators into the garden, which will increase the amount of fruit you'll get. Flowers can also help control some pests. For example, marigolds produce substances that deter some types of nematodes, which can be particularly damaging to root crops. Edibles and flowers can also be very attractive planted together. Scarlet runner beans, 'Bright Lights' Swiss chard, and artichokes are just a few of the vegetables that look really stunning in an ornamental garden.

High-Density Planting

If you're interested in growing fruit trees but have limited space, there are techniques that can still give you the orchard effect you desire. High-density planting includes several ways to plant and prune fruit trees to produce bigger and longer harvests by including cross-pollinizers and varieties that bear at earlier and later times. The most common methods are planting two, three, or four trees in one hole; espaliering trees against a wall or fence; and planting multiple trees in hedgerow. For diagrams of high-density plantings, check out the California Rare Fruit Growers' (CRFG) website at www.crfg. org/tidbits/byo-examples.html.

Another technique for multiplying your harvest is to graft cuttings from compatible cross-pollinizing varieties onto one tree. Some nurseries offer pre-grafted multiple-variety trees (apple trees are the ones most commonly sold this way), but you can also do the grafting yourself. Every winter the California Rare Fruit Growers local chapters hold a Scion Exchange where you can find cuttings from a wide range of fruit trees, as well as information and demonstrations on how to graft. Contact CRFG (www.crfg.org) for information.

Dwarf Varieties

While you can prune standard-sized trees to stay small, it takes a lot of pruning and real dedication to keep them that size. It is much easier to plant dwarf varieties. Some dwarf varieties are genetic dwarfs—they have been bred to be a smaller size. Most, however, are varieties selected for superior fruit that are grafted onto dwarf rootstock.

Dwarf trees allow for easier harvesting and pruning. Be aware, though, that "dwarf" can be a relative term. Some dwarfs top out at 8 feet, others at 15 or 20 feet. Be sure to check the expected height for that variety before you buy.

Container Gardening

The simple truth is you don't need a patch of open ground to plant an edible garden. You can grow most of the edibles in this book in containers. You could even have an orchard of fruit trees—all in containers.

Container gardening can solve, or at

least work around, many problems. If your garden soil is diseased or contaminated or just not as healthy as you'd like, you can get around those problems with containers filled with fresh potting soil and compost. If you have physical limitations that make it difficult for you to bend or kneel on the ground, containers can give you easier access to the plants. Soil in containers warms up before soil in the ground, giving heat-loving seeds and seedlings a jump on growing. Containers can add color and style to your garden, provide mobility and flexibility to your plantings, and increase your available planting space.

But let's also discuss a few of the challenges of container gardening. Container plantings need more frequent watering and can suffer greatly in extreme heat. The salts in potted soils build up over time and need to be flushed from the containers occasionally before they become toxic for the plants. Container-grown trees will need to be taken out of their pots every three or four years and root pruned before repotting in fresh soil to keep the root system healthy and prevent the trees from becoming root-bound.

Containers can be almost anything large enough to hold the mature root system for the intended plant and can be made of clay, wood, plastic, fiberglass, or other materials. For larger plants, you may want to use lighter-weight containers in case they have to be moved. Another good idea is to put casters on large containers to make them more mobile.

Timing

The time of year for planting different fruits and vegetables is critical to success. Those times are tied to each plant's needs regarding temperature. Plant too soon and some plants will be vulnerable to frosts and freezes. Plant too late and they will not have enough warm days to grow and set fruit.

Knowing the first and last average frost dates for your area will help you determine when to plant. For an initial planning guide, check the average dates for frosts listed in the following box. For dates more specific to your locale, there are a number of websites that give frost and freeze dates by zip codes. One of the best sites I've found is http://davesgarden.com/guides/freeze-frost-dates. Armed with this information, you can plan out when to start seeds indoors and when you can safely move them outdoors.

California Average Last Frost/First Frost Dates

To use this chart, find the city nearest you. Adjust the dates accordingly, depending on whether your climate is cooler or warmer. Remember that the dates provided are averages only and will vary from year to year.

City	Last Frost (spring)	First Frost (fall)
Bakersfield	February 21	November 25
Eureka	March 10	November 18
Fresno	March 14	November 19
Los Angeles	January 3	December 28
Marysville	February 21	November 21
Palm Springs	January 18	December 18
Pasadena	February 3	December 13
Red Bluff	March 6	December 5
Riverside	March 6	November 26
Sacramento	February 6	December 10
San Diego	Never!	Never!
San Francisco	January 7	December 29
San Jose	February 10	January 6
Santa Barbara	January 22	December 19
Santa Rosa	April 10	November 3

Timing is also an issue when planting trees. The best time to plant deciduous trees is when they are dormant. With evergreen trees, such as citrus, there is no real dormant period, so the best planting time becomes whenever the tree will be least stressed. That usually means when the temperatures are not extreme—not in a heat wave, and not in times of potential frost. Planting when there's no risk of heat or cold stress will allow the tree to become established and healthy before it has to endure those difficulties. The result will be a stronger tree.

STARTING AT THE BEGINNING WITH SEEDS

Given the choice between buying seedlings in six-packs or 4-inch pots or starting the plants myself from seed, I'll almost always choose the latter. There are a lot of advantages to growing from seed, but the most obvious one is cost. Seeds are by far the most inexpensive way to grow. In addition, with seeds you'll have a much wider range of plant varieties from which to choose, including interesting heirloom varieties that you will never find in the stores. And I've often found that plants I've grown from seed in my garden become better established than transplanted seedlings from the nursery.

But the truth is I just love planting seeds and watching them grow. It is fascinating to watch the seedlings emerge, then unfold their true leaves and reach for the light. Many people seem to think that growing plants from seed is complicated, but for most vegetables and herbs, it is really quite simple. It's just a matter of creating the right environment for the seedlings to start their lives.

Direct Sow Versus Transplants

In the plant profiles that follow in this book and on seed packets, you'll find information about whether the seeds should be started indoors or planted directly in the ground. There are a few factors that determine whether a plant is a good candidate for direct sowing or not, including the germination time and the type of root system the plant has. Plants that are slow to germinate may benefit from the head start of growing indoors. On the other hand, some plants have taproots or delicate root systems that don't tolerate transplanting well and are better off taking their chances outdoors right from the beginning. Some plants can go either way, but starting indoors will give them the advantage of a few additional weeks of growing before temperatures permit moving them outdoors.

For those plants that can be direct sown, a good deal of their survival depends on how well you prepare the ground for them. The planting bed should be free of weeds, rocks, and other debris and the soil loose enough to accommodate tender roots. For root crops such as carrots and parsnips, be sure the ground is loosened and all rocks removed to the depth the roots will grow. Planting these crops in soil that is rocky will lead to roots that are forked and deformed as they try to grow around the stones. It's always helpful to work compost into the soil before sowing seeds. It helps the soil retain moisture and has nutrients the seedlings will need as soon as the roots develop.

Once the soil is loose enough, smooth it out with a rake and trace out a seeding plan in the ground. If you're planting in rows, use a rake handle or the narrow side of a board to press the row into the soil. Drop in the seeds at the recommended spacing and cover with soil. A rule of thumb is to cover seeds to the same depth as the width of the seed, so tiny seeds are scantly covered and bigger seeds are planted more deeply.

Some seeds, like lettuces, for example, can be broadcast, or sprinkled generally over a prepared area. With really fine seeds, it can be hard to tell if you're distributing them evenly enough. A good trick is to mix the seeds with horticultural sand or vermiculite and sprinkle the mixture over the soil. The sand or vermiculite is easier to see and you'll be able to get a better broadcast.

Tamp down on the seeded area well to make sure the seeds and soil are in good contact and there are no big air pockets left. Water the seeded area well with a fine mist. Be sure to label what you've planted.

Did you get the feeling someone was watching you while you were planting? You were right—birds. And they're waiting for you to go inside so they can swoop down and steal the seeds you just planted. To spoil their

plans, you can put inverted plastic strawberry baskets over the larger seeds, or use floating row covers over the entire seeded area. Row covers allow sunlight and moisture to get through, but keep pests away and protect tender seedlings in case of a late light frost.

Sowing Seeds Indoors

For plants that can be transplanted, you can get a jump on the growing season by sowing seeds indoors. The optimum conditions for starting seeds involves grow lights and heating mats, but most seeds can be started easily under less than optimum conditions. Some things you can't compromise on, however— sterile soil and growing containers, adequate moisture, and warmth.

Let's start with the soil. It's not necessary to use "seed-starting" mixes. It is necessary, though, to use soil that is sterile. A seed-starter mix is good because it contains sphagnum moss, which is a natural fungicide to help prevent "damping off," a common destroyer of newly sprouted seedlings. There are methods for sterilizing soil yourself, but honestly, it's not worth it. Just buy bags of good-quality potting mix. I prefer to mix it in equal proportions with perlite, a naturally occurring, lightweight volcanic material that helps improve the drainage. While seedlings definitely need adequate water, tender roots will drown if not in a well-draining mix.

But what should you grow the seeds in? There are many options. To plant seeds individually, you can use recycled plastic six-packs and small

(2-inch or 4-inch) pots from the nursery or even yogurt containers (with holes cut in the bottom for drainage). Some people use egg cartons, but I don't think they are deep enough to give the roots much room. Other people use peat pots that can be planted directly in the ground, but I've found that in sandy, fast-draining soils like I have, the peat decomposes way too slowly, keeping the roots inhibited. And you should definitely not use peat plugs to start seeds in. (Peat has all the wrong drainage properties for seeds.) Whatever container you use, make sure it is completely clean; wash it with a 10% bleach solution to make sure it is free of bacteria as well.

Some people prefer to plant in flats, but that can make transplanting a little more stressful for the plants that have to have their roots detangled. One way I've found to get around that problem is to make soil blocks in flats. Some of my most successful seed starting has been done in soil blocks in those clear plastic clamshell boxes you get take-out food in. (Having the lid to keep it closed keeps in more moisture.) You can buy handy-dandy gadgets that form soil blocks quickly in multiples, and if you're starting a lot of seeds, that may be a good investment for you. Since I usually start seeds a few small batches at a time, I just use a square 2-inch plastic pot as the form. All you do is prepare your soil mix and moisten it enough so that it will hold together in a clump in your hand. Fill your soil block form with the mix, packing it in tightly and then releasing it upside

down into the flat. Keep repeating until the flat is filled with blocks that are touching on all sides but not firmly packed together. Use a pencil or chopstick to make an indentation in each block and drop in the seed at the proper depth. Cover the seed with soil and water lightly.

Before seedlings emerge, what seeds need more than light is warmth. Professional propagators use heat mats for that purpose, but you can improvise. Find a warm spot in your house and set up the seed trays there. I've started seeds on top of my refrigerator and on a cookie sheet placed over a radiator—that worked great, actually! As soon as the seedlings emerge, however, move them to a place where they can get the best light possible. Insufficient light will cause seedlings to get leggy, a weakness that some plants never really recover from. If you notice your seedlings getting leggy, add additional light (lower-hanging lights just above the plants) and direct a fan blowing gently over the seedlings for an hour or two each day. The movement caused by the breeze helps strengthen the stems. If weather permits, start hardening off (see the next section) the seedlings as soon as possible.

In addition to soil, containers, and heat and light, the last thing that seeds absolutely must have is consistent watering. While many mature plants can handle the stress of drying out and come back from it when they finally do get water, seedlings just can't. Check the soil daily; it should be moist, but not waterlogged (too much water is as damaging as too little). Add water as needed.

Moving Outdoors

Once your seedlings are big enough for transplanting and the last average frost date has passed, it's time to get them ready for life outside. This process, called *hardening off*, is a little like sending your kids off to school—you want to send them out for just a short time each day and let them get used to the new environment slowly.

Find a spot outside that is protected from wind and animals that can knock them around, and leave them there, first for an hour or two, and then for longer and longer periods of time. Indirect light is best at first, and then gradually work them toward full sun exposure. Since the plants are still very tender, check them when you bring them in each day to make sure they aren't getting attacked by bugs.

If at first you're not noticing any discernible difference in your plants as you begin hardening them off, then you know you're doing it right. But as the amount of time the plants spend outdoors increases, you should notice the plants looking a bit more vigorous, with thickening stems and fuller foliage. That's when it's time to transplant.

Plant them in their new location, disturbing the root systems as little as possible, and water them well. If after a few days you see signs of transplant shock (wilting or dieback), try trimming the plant back by as much as a third. Keep watering and give it a chance to redirect some of its energy back toward the roots. With a little bit of luck, the plants will settle into their new home and get growing.

Saving Seeds

Farmers have been saving seeds since the earliest days of agriculture, but we've learned a thing or two along the way to make the process more efficient. There are good reasons for saving seeds, the first of which is the money it saves. Instead of having to purchase new seed year after year for your favorite crops, often at $1.50 or more a pack, you can save the seed of the plants you know you were able to grow successfully. Even the best seed companies have occasional crop failures, and saving your own seeds will ensure that you'll have the seeds you want each year.

Another reason to save seeds is to be able to participate in seed exchanges. These seed swaps are becoming more and more common lately, and you can find them through gardening groups, on the Internet, or maybe even your local library. My city library recently started a seed library where you can take out seeds contributed by other gardeners and deposit seeds that you have saved. As with seeds saved from your own garden, you can be fairly confident that seeds from a local seed exchange will grow well in your garden.

To collect seeds, you have to be willing to sacrifice the fruit on one or two plants. Save seeds from your healthiest and most vigorous plants; after all, you want to carry on the genetic characteristics of the best of the crop. After the fruit has fully matured, open up the fruit and collect the seed. Wash the seed well to make sure all of the flesh from the fruit has been removed, then spread the seed out in a single layer on paper towels on a cookie sheet or plate. Put the seeds somewhere out of direct light but with good air circulation and let the seed dry *completely*. When you think the seed is completely dry, spread them out on a fresh paper towel and dry them another day just to make sure. When they really are completely dry, package them for storage. Ultimately, seeds should be stored in an airtight container, but you can package the different varieties in envelopes, plastic containers, or Ziploc bags, and then store those labeled packages together in an airtight container. If you want to get fancy, you can do a Google search for "seed pack templates" and find all kinds of designs for seed envelopes to download and print from your computer. Once the seeds are all packed, store the container in your refrigerator. Heat and sunlight can damage seeds, so the refrigerator provides the best, most consistent climate for seed storage.

If you're wondering how long you can store seeds, there's no one answer to that. Some seeds simply have a longer shelf life than do others. But generally speaking, and assuming you've stored them properly, you can expect corn, leek, rhubarb, parsnip, and parsley seed to last a couple years. Asparagus, bean, Brussels sprouts, cabbage, carrot, cauliflower, celery, kale, lettuce, okra, pea, pepper, radish, spinach, turnip, and watermelon seed can last two to three years, and tomato, eggplant, and cucumber seed might last three to five years.

To test whether stored seeds are still viable, moisten a paper towel and spread about ten seeds over it. Fold up the paper towel and seal it in a Ziploc bag. Check the seeds every day to see how many have germinated. If half of them germinate, that's a 50% germination rate. Then you know that you have to sow at least twice as many seeds as the number of plants you want to grow. You can adjust the number of seeds you plant up or down based on what your germination rate is.

A word of warning about saving seeds from fruit: Many fruits, such as apples, for example, do not grow true from seed. You can plant the seed and grow an apple tree from it, but the fruit you'll get from it will not be a genetic match to the fruit the seed came from and will most likely be inferior to that original fruit. If you want a dependable fruit tree, you need to buy a grafted variety from a nursery or learn to graft one yourself.

Saving seed is a great way to keep the success stories in your garden ongoing. With your own saved seed, you'll know that you're planting not only your favorite crops, but also the ones that have performed well in your soil and climate and have been spared the pesticide contamination that most commercial seeds have been subjected to. You'll know exactly what you're planting and what you can expect from it. Seeds saved from hybrid plants will not turn out the same as their parents and may not even germinate at all. It's best to save open-pollinated—and heirloom—seeds.

CREATING THE PERFECT SOIL

Perhaps you live in an area with dark, nutrient-rich loam. When you squeeze a handful of soil, it forms a clod that then crumbles in your hand. When you breathe it in, it doesn't smell like salt or chemicals; it smells fresh, moist, and alive. Lucky you! From a gardener's perspective, sitting on good soil is like sitting on a pile of gold. Odds are, however, that your soil is less than perfect. You may have sandy soil that has the benefit of good drainage, but is deficient in nutrients. Or you may have clay soil that turns to hard rock in the summer and waterlogged muck in the rainy season. Maybe your soil is highly acidic or highly alkaline. Whatever your soil conditions, there are simple ways to improve them. It may take some time and diligence to work your way toward having that lovely loam in which most fruits and vegetables thrive, but it can be done.

Keeping It Loose

Good soil is loose soil. Good soil crumbles in your hand but doesn't slip through your fingers like sand through an hourglass. Good soil yields to a shovel rather than meeting it the way cement meets a toothpick. This may not describe your soil as it is now, but your soil can become loose, or friable, as gardeners like to call it.

Many people think the way to get loose soil is to get out a rototiller and till it. Double-digging is another technique people have used. These techniques work, but they can also break down the structure of the soil, and they're usually not necessary, unless you have very rocky soil. Working compost into the soil and adding a layer of organic mulch on top will, over time, accomplish the same thing as rototilling, and it will improve the soil structure rather than destroying it.

If you have heavy clay soil, there is another step you can take to make your soil looser and more workable. Buy a few bags of gypsum (calcium sulfate dehydrate) and spread it liberally over your soil, like a light dusting of snow. Then spread a few inches of an organic mulch over that and water. Keep watering regularly—some soils will take longer—and in a few months, you will find that your hard clay has become friable. This is not a one-time fix; in time it may become hard again and you will have to repeat this procedure.

For sandy soil that is too loose, compost, or any organic matter, and mulch are all you need.

How Not to Drown or Dry Out Your Plants

We tend to think of soil as a solid, but in fact it is highly oxygenated—or at least it should be. In dense clay soils, water drains slowly, pushing out the oxygen and leaving delicate roots unable to reach it—in other words, drowning. In sandy soils, on the other hand, there is so much space between soil particles that water passes through it quickly, giving roots a quick drink but no consistent moisture, so they dry out faster. In a healthy loam, drainage is fast enough to allow roots to still get oxygen but slow enough that they get all the moisture they need.

In some extreme cases, you may need to install French drains or pipes to handle severe drainage problems. But often enough humus is what makes the difference in soil drainage. Humus is organic matter that has broken down completely and when combined with clay or sandy soil, it not only adds nutrients, it also improves the drainage. You add humus to your soil by working in compost, aged manure, rotted leaves, grass clippings, and other organic matter. It doesn't improve the soil overnight, and you may need to look to raised beds, container planting, and other techniques to get you through to the day when your soil drains properly. Over time you should see your soil drain more efficiently as the overall soil quality improves.

Acidic Versus Alkaline: Getting the Right pH

Various pH numbers get tossed around a lot in garden books, and it's easy to think that it ruins the fun of gardening by dragging chemistry—yes, that subject most of us barely survived in high school—into it. But pH isn't all that complicated. Here's all you really need to know: pH level refers to the acidity or alkalinity (also called the basicity) of the soil. It works on a scale of 0 to 14 with the midpoint, 7, being *neutral soil*, equally balanced between acidity and alkalinity. Soil that measures between 7 and 14 is alkaline or basic soil. Soil that measures from 0 to 7 is acidic soil. Fruits and vegetables tend to prefer soil that falls between 6.0 and 7.5 on the pH scale.

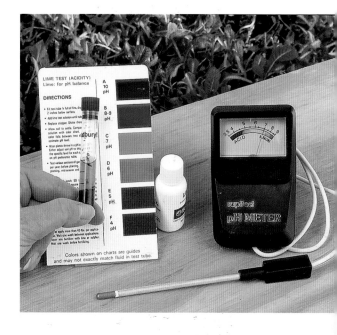

Why should you care about the soil's pH level? Because when the pH is either too low or too high, it adversely affects how nutrients become available to plants. Having a pH level that is too low or too high probably won't kill your plants, but it could cause them to lack vigor simply because they are starved for nutrients that are present but not available for their use.

To find out what your soil's pH level is, go to a nursery or garden center and buy a pH test kit. They cost only a few dollars and are simple to use. They include a chart to compare your results to so you can quickly get your pH number.

If your test indicates that your soil is too acidic (lower than 6.0), you can make it more alkaline by adding pulverized lime or wood ash. If your test indicates that your soil is too alkaline (higher than 7.5), you can make it more acidic by adding sphagnum peat, sulfur, aluminum sulfate, or organic mulches, particularly mulching with pine needles. Don't go overboard in adding any of these amendments. Your plants won't appreciate having the pH level changed too drastically or too quickly.

Growing Deep Roots

It makes no difference whether you're planting radishes or pecan trees, roots needs to grow *down*. In California, where some housing developments were built on a few scant inches of imported topsoil, that can sometimes be a problem. So how deep is your topsoil? The only way to find out is to take a shovel and dig. You may find that the only way you can provide your plants with enough loose soil to grow healthy root systems is to garden *up*, by building raised beds or using lasagna-style planting methods. Over time, you can change not only the quality of your topsoil but also its depth. And your plants will thank you for it.

Nematodes: Friend or Foe?

Sometimes the reason that plants thrive or die has something to do with an agent you'll never actually be able to see, at least not with the naked eye.

Lurking in your soil are microscopic worms, some of which are beneficial and some of which are parasitic. The beneficial nematodes are predators of other soil pests, like cutworms. Parasitic nematodes, such as root knot nematodes, suck the sap from roots, inhibiting a plant's ability to take in nutrients, and can also spread viruses. If you have a serious problem with nematodes, you can steam or solarize the soil, but that will kill the beneficials as well as the parasites.

A better approach is to try to achieve a balance with nematodes. Do this by planting nematode- and disease-resistant plant varieties and by rotating crops annually. Adding organic matter or planting cover crops that fix nitrogen into the soil also helps keep the parasitic nematode population in check and the soil healthy.

Feeding the Soil

Think of your soil as a smorgasbord for your plants. Do you know what nutrients it has to offer? It's easy enough to find out. Once again, your local nursery or garden center has soil test kits that will tell you how much of the major nutrients or micronutrients your soil has. Or you can take the standard soil test offered by the University of Massachusetts Amherst

(www.umass.edu/soiltest/list_of_services.htm). For only $10 they'll measure the pH, major nutrients, heavy metals, and more. With that information in hand, you'll be in good shape to give your soil exactly what it needs and nothing more. That means you won't be wasting money on unneeded fertilizers that just wash off into the local waters. I also like that this test measures heavy metals, because you shouldn't grow edibles in soil that is heavily contaminated with these metals.

Once you've determined what nutrients your soil needs, you can find the fertilizer that will supply it. The three main nutrients that plants need are nitrogen (N) for green growth, phosphorus (P) for blooming and fruiting, and potassium (K) for overall vigor. When you look at fertilizer packages, you will often see three numbers, such as 10-0-10 or 5-20-10. Those are the N-P-K indicators that tell you what the proportions are of each nutrient in that fertilizer. If you want a high-nitrogen fertilizer, look for a higher first number. If you want to encourage fruiting, look for a higher middle number. Often you want a little bit of everything; in those cases look for a *balanced fertilizer*, indicated by the same number for each nutrient, for example 10-10-10.

Fertilizers can be organic (made of plant or animal products) or inorganic (made of synthetic chemicals). From the plant's point of view, there isn't much difference. Organic nitrogen and synthetic nitrogen work just the same. But there are other differences to consider. While organic

fertilizers, such as compost, manure, and fish emulsion, improve the biodiversity of the soil, they can also contain pathogens and their nutrient values can be more variable. On the other hand, inorganic fertilizers may not replace trace nutrients in the soil and are produced in ways that are not sustainable.

Whatever fertilizer you use, you should be sure to water plants well *before and after* applying the fertilizer. Fertilizing a plant that isn't hydrated will cause it to burn. Apply the fertilizer in the amount recommended on the package—don't overdo it! Follow the recommendations given in the plant profiles later in this book for how often and at what time of year to fertilize plants.

For fruit trees, keep in mind that roots don't just grow down, they also grow out, so you need to apply the fertilizer in a way that will reach all the roots. The bulk of the root system for a tree will be contained within the *dripline* of the tree. The drip line refers to the perimeter around the area that is covered by the entire canopy of the tree. I have a Santa Rosa weeping plum tree that is about 7 feet wide—3½ feet on either side of the trunk. If I drew a circle that runs 3½ feet out from the trunk all the way around the tree, that would be the drip line. To fertilize that tree adequately, I should apply the appropriate amount of fertilizer evenly within that drip line.

Providing the necessary nutrients for your plants and ensuring the soil is in good health is one of the most important things you can do to achieve a good harvest.

WATERING &
OTHER NECESSITIES

Water is a California gardener's biggest headache. Since most of the state has dry summers, growing summer fruits and vegetables means a constant effort to ensure they are getting sufficient water. And given the variations in soils from one region to another, drainage can become a problem as well.

As if that isn't enough to concern you, keep in mind that it's not just a matter of how much water you give your plants, but at what time of day and by what method. Water at the wrong time and you'll lose a good deal of the moisture to evaporation. Water in the wrong way and you could contribute to the spread of fungal diseases.

Recent droughts have made Californians very water-conscious, and some have started to use various conservation methods. That can be a big benefit to your garden, but any water you use on edible plants must be free of chemicals. That means exercising some additional care with the water you save and recycle.

Whether you have an elaborate, timer-enforced irrigation system or water your entire garden by hand, the goal is the same—to get the proper amount of water to the plants' roots without wasting any and without spreading disease. And there are really only a few guidelines you need to keep in mind to accomplish that.

The Basics of Watering

Before you get to the question of how you should water, it helps to understand some basic tips about watering:

- ➤ The best time to water is early morning, just before dawn. Water will have time to penetrate the soil before it can evaporate, and plants will have the moisture they need during the heat of day. Also, roots are less likely to rot when they haven't been sitting in water throughout the night.
- ➤ The best method of watering is drip irrigation or soaker hoses, which get the water directly to the root systems with little or no evaporation and no splashing water to carry fungal diseases.
- ➤ Consistency matters. Inconsistent watering can stress a plant and cause fruit to split. Blossom end rot in tomatoes can also be caused by inconsistent watering.
- ➤ If you recycle water from your household (gray water), do not use it on your edible plants. Use the gray water on ornamental plants and lawns, and save the fresh water for your fruits and vegetables.
- ➤ Infrequent and deep watering beats frequent light watering. Why? Because deep watering encourages deeper, healthier root systems. For fruit trees in particular, a deep root system will lead to better overall health and fruit production.

With this information in hand, as well as an understanding of your soil type and particular plants' water needs, you can create an optimum schedule for watering.

Watering for Maximum Efficiency

Beyond having a regular watering schedule, there are a few extra things you can do to help your plants make the most of the available water.

For starters, mulch! A 3- to 4-inch layer of organic mulch (wood chips, compost, straw, pine needles, newspaper, cardboard, and so forth) minimizes evaporation, keeping more of the water in the ground where it can get to the roots. Mulching is one of the most effective things you can do to keep your garden healthy.

Next, be vigilant about weeds, which rob your plants of water and nutrients. Pull weeds as soon as you see them and use mulch to help suppress them. One added benefit of using drip irrigation rather than using a sprinkler to water everything indiscriminately is that you're not encouraging more weed growth. Instead, the water goes directly to the roots of your fruits and vegetables.

Use hydrozoning, a system of grouping plants together by their water needs. If all the plants that need heavy watering are grouped in one area and all the ones that need infrequent deep watering are in another, you can give each group just the water it needs and no more. Also, make sure you water the whole root area. For trees, that means watering the entire space within the dripline of the tree, not just immediately surrounding the trunk.

Lastly, if you have an irrigation system installed, make sure it's operating at peak efficiency. Check drip emitters or sprinkler heads to make sure they aren't clogged and that they are properly aimed so the water goes to the plants, not the sidewalk. Use the system's timer to water early in the morning and for the proper intervals. Some of the newer, more advanced irrigation control systems even download satellite weather information to adjust the watering schedule to what your garden really needs.

Irrigation Techniques and Rain Harvesting

There are three general methods of irrigating your garden. The first is drip irrigation, which uses narrow aboveground tubing and drip emitters to deliver water in small amounts to the precise locations you want in the garden. This is the most efficient irrigation system because it gets the water directly at the roots and the least amount of water is lost to evaporation. This kind of system needs to be monitored regularly to make sure emitters are working correctly and also to ensure that that the water is not dripping directly against the plant stems or tree trunks, which can cause crown rot.

Another type of irrigation is a sprinkler system. These systems use underground pipes and sprinkler heads (stationary or

pop-up) to spray water in a certain direction. Sprinklers use considerably more water than drip systems—gallons per minute as opposed to gallons per hour. They also lose more water to evaporation, and because they spray at or over plants, they can leave foliage wet, which can be conducive to the spread of fungal diseases. They can also cause a lot of runoff because they can deliver water faster than the ground can absorb it. You can control runoff by setting the system to go on and off for short intervals, allowing the water time to penetrate the soil.

If you don't have an irrigation system in place, that leaves hand watering. While hand watering does use more water than a drip system and leaves water on the foliage, it has the advantage of getting the water directly to the intended areas in easy-to-control amounts. It can be very time-consuming, of course, especially for a larger garden. One way to minimize the hands-on time of hand watering as well as maximize the water efficiency is to use soaker hoses. These are either flat hoses with holes on top or round hoses that seem to ooze water all around. By winding the hoses throughout the garden bed, you can deliver the water close to the root systems in much the same way that drip emitters do.

One of the simplest and most common water conservation techniques used is very low-tech: rain barrels. Large waterproof barrels strategically placed around your house to collect water from rain gutters can save many gallons of water that you can use for your garden. If you live in a region with a fair amount of rain throughout the year, rain barrels are great, but in dry-summer regions, they're of limited use. They fill up fast in the rain and the water gets used up fast. And then there may be weeks or even months where it doesn't rain again and the barrels just sit there empty, taking up space. And there's another problem—rain that runs off roofs may pick up bacteria from birds and insects as well as chemicals used in some roofing materials. That water should not be used on edible plants. As with gray water (from washing machines), rain barrel water should be used on ornamental plants only so that you can save the fresh water for the fruits and vegetables.

Basic Tools

Aside from the equipment you need to water your garden, you should have a few other tools on hand to manage your garden. There are a lot of goodies out there on the market that will tempt you, and a person could easily go broke buying all the gardening stuff that retailers want to sell you. The truth is, about 90% of it isn't necessary, and about 50% of it isn't even all that helpful. But there are some tools that are very hard to do without, and a few others that, while not vital, are awfully helpful to have. Here are the essential and near-essential garden tools I'd recommend.

Shovel

No doubt about it, a good shovel is a necessity. Shovels can be long-handled or short-handled, and round-pointed or square-pointed. Round-pointed shovels are for digging; square-pointed shovels are better for collecting and lifting material rather than for digging. Don't cheap out on this—a good shovel should last you many years.

Trowel

Trowels are for digging small holes for transplanting or planting bulbs. Get one with a very sturdy blade (cheaper ones will bend easily) and a comfortable grip.

Pruner and Lopper

My favorite tool is my set of bypass hand-pruners. There are other types of pruner blades—anvil and parrot-beak—but bypass pruners, which work like scissors, are the best for cutting small branches without crushing the stems. Be sure to get pruners that fit well in your hand (there are different sizes and different styles for lefties), and it also helps to get a holster for it that clips on a belt or pocket.

To cut larger branches (wider than a finger), you need a pair of loppers. Loppers are like heavy-duty pruners with extended handles, but you need two hands to operate them.

Rake

When it's time to prep a vegetable bed at the beginning of the season or clear it out at the end of the season, a rake becomes essential. A good steel rake can take out small rocks and smooth a bed for sowing seeds, or clear away rotten fruit and leaves that would become a breeding ground for pests and diseases.

Garden Fork

Garden forks have many uses, but particularly for harvesting root crops like potatoes, beets, and onions, they are the best way to lift the roots without damaging them. Garden forks are also useful for breaking up heavy soils to begin preparing beds.

Hose

A good hose is a worthwhile investment. While cheaper hoses will get the job done, the annoyance factor will be huge. Cheap hoses kink and twist and split and leak. To avoid those irritations, get a hose made of rubber, preferably with brass couplings to attach it to the faucet and other hoses. A pistol-type nozzle with multiple spray patterns is really useful as well.

If you don't have drip irrigation installed in your garden, the next best option is a soaker hose. Often made of recycled rubber tires, soaker hoses connect to a faucet or regular hose and emit droplets of water down the length of the hose. It's a good way to get the water directly to the root systems with minimal evaporation and without splashing water on the foliage, which can spread fungal diseases.

Garden Cart

A garden cart or wheelbarrow can spare your back a lot of strain when it's time to haul in bags of potting soil or fertilizer. The first few years I gardened I didn't have one, and I probably spent enough in chiropractor appointments to have bought a couple of garden carts. Learn from my pain!

Composter

When you have a vegetable garden, there are two things you can be sure of: 1) you're going to be producing a lot of green waste, and 2) you're going to need a lot of compost. You might as well have a composter to put your green waste in to create your own compost. Composters can be as simple as wire cages or boxes built out of wooden pallets, but some local utility agencies offer terrific deals on heavy-duty composters and worm bins that save you the trouble of constructing a compost bin. Whatever you use, a composter will keep a lot of green waste out of the landfill and put it to work right in your own garden in the form of healthy organic compost.

Hat

A wide-brim hat is an often overlooked but really essential accessory for gardeners. Skin cancer is too high a price to pay for a great garden. Daily exposure to the sun takes a toll on your face, and an uncovered head puts you at a greater risk for sunstroke. It doesn't really matter what kind of hat you get; the best kind is the kind that you will actually wear.

Gloves

Some people really don't like wearing gloves, but I still think every gardener should have a good pair on hand. There are some plants, such as spiny squash plants, that just aren't easy to handle with bare hands. If you are going to use gloves, don't bother with those quaint little cotton gloves you see at the hardware stores. Get the sturdiest but most dexterous ones you can find. I've used Atlas gloves and Ethel gloves, and would recommend both, but there are others out there that will work for you as well.

Tools for Maintaining Tools

There's no point in investing in good tools if you aren't going to take care of them. Tools need to be regularly cleaned, sharpened, and oiled if you want them to last. One of the best tips I ever got was to keep a bucket or small trash can filled with sand and a couple quarts of motor oil. When you finish using a shovel or trowel or garden fork, all you have to do is brush off the dirt and then plunge it into the sand a few times before putting it away. The sand cleans and sharpens the blades and the oil lubricates to prevent it from rusting.

For pruners and loppers, keep a sharpening stone on hand. A few quick swipes of the stone give you a sharp blade. Sharp blades make clean cuts and clean cuts are less susceptible to disease. Pruners should also be oiled periodically to keep them moving smoothly and resistant to rust. And here's the best tip of all: Keep a container of disinfectant wipes with you whenever you're pruning. After you finish pruning each plant or tree, wipe your pruners and loppers down with the disinfectant so that you won't be spreading bacteria or fungi onto other plants.

PESTS & DISEASES

This is the part of the book that's similar to those long lists of potential side effects that you get with prescription medicines. The unfortunate truth is that the same wonderful climate that we Californians enjoy that makes growing food so easy also makes a welcome environment for many pests and diseases. Many of them are more of a nuisance than a serious threat, but there are a few bugs and diseases that can be extremely damaging and difficult to eradicate or even control, particularly if you're trying to avoid toxic chemicals. In most cases, however, there are simple steps that will keep your plants' defenses up and their enemies at bay.

BUGS

Bugs! They can be the bane of your existence or the cavalry riding in to save the day (and the crop). We could never account for all the insects, aboveground and below, that live or at least pass through our gardens. Like the criminal element of the garden, some bugs will make their presence known in very unpleasant ways. Others are like busy businessmen making deals and swapping goods—we depend upon them for pollination, without which we'd have no fruits or vegetables at all. Still others act like the garden's security guards, ready to stare down and, if necessary, eat the thug bugs that are eating our plants. It's a complicated world.

California's problem with destructive bugs isn't as serious as some of the more tropical areas, but bugs are still treated as a significant threat here. The reason? The state has a $36 billion agriculture industry. California farmers can't afford to let an infestation get out of hand, so the state is vigilant about containing any real threat posed by an invading insect and has in the past instituted spraying programs and quarantines to eradicate or control problems with the Mediterranean fruit fly, the light brown apple moth, and the Asian citrus psyllid, to name just a few.

But most bug problems are not that serious. And it is important that our responses to any insect problem be proportional to the actual threat. One of the main reasons that you're growing your own food is probably that you'd like to eat less contaminated food than what you're likely to find in the store. That means you don't want to go nuclear on every bug that deigns to feed on your tender little plants. Your garden is a complex biological community, and almost any attack you launch against insects will certainly affect more than the targeted bug and the plant it's living on.

The law of unintended consequences says that any intervention in a complex situation will result in unanticipated and sometimes undesirable outcomes. The same controls that kill pest insects also kill beneficial insects. That's an unintended consequence. The same controls that kill pest insects can also lead to their building up a genetic immunity to that control so that we create super-bugs that we need even more lethal controls to kill. That's one heck of an unintended consequence.

Gardeners who practice sustainable gardening methods believe that we should have more of a "let's all get along" approach to pest control. This is called *integrated pest management (IPM)*, and its goal is to reduce or eliminate the use of pesticides by practicing prevention, observation, and, when necessary, intervention to control significant pest damage. For the home gardener, this is by far the safest and in many ways the easiest strategy. It means accepting minor bug damage but foregoing the most toxic weapons of mass destruction to combat every little pest. By using biological controls, mechanical controls, and good sanitation practices, we can in most cases keep our gardens healthy while we keep the thugs of the insect world in check.

Good Bugs/Bad Bugs

As a fairly girly girl, it took me a while to come to terms with the idea that not all bugs are bad. Except for the obvious ladybugs and butterflies, I

wasn't inclined to give any of them a pass. But I've since learned to welcome certain bugs in my garden and encourage them to keep coming back.

First, let's welcome the pollinators—God bless every one of them! All kinds of bees, butterflies, moths, beetles, and even ants pollinate the flowers necessary for fruit to set. (Yes, even beetles and ants, regulars on the pest hit list, do us the favor of spreading a little pollen as they weave their path of destruction!) Without them, we might as well hang up our trowels and call it quits.

Then there are the predator insects that keep the pests in check. Ladybugs eat huge numbers of aphids and other small insects that suck on plants. Trichogramma wasps, or stingless wasps, ingeniously inject their eggs into the eggs of codling moths, European corn borers, and other pests. Their larvae then consume the contents of the other eggs, limiting the pest population. Praying mantises

are voracious predators and will consume all kinds of insects from aphids on up. They are effective controls for serious infestations, but if there are not enough pests to satisfy them, they'll consume other beneficial insects as well.

These are just a few examples of the insects that we should encourage in our gardens but would also be killed by some of the heavier-handed chemical controls we might use. With that in mind, let's look at more environmentally friendly tactics to employ.

Mechanical Controls

Let's start with the simplest and easiest-on-the-environment methods of pest control:

- ➤ Handpicking caterpillars and beetles off your plants is both effective and immediate. Wear a glove if the "ick" factor bothers you at all, and drown the bugs in a jar of water and dish detergent before disposing of them in the trash.
- ➤ For tinier bugs such as aphids and scale, a blast of water from the hose will wash them away in an instant.
- ➤ Many bugs such as aphids, scale, and mealybugs become a problem because there is an existing ant problem. Ants basically "farm" these insects for their "honeydew" secretions. If you control the ants, you will have an easier time controlling the other bugs. One way to keep ants off fruit trees is to use a product such as Tanglefoot, a sticky paste that you paint around the base of a tree to keep ants from climbing up.

- ➤ Diatomaceous earth (DE) is a good barrier for crawling insects. This natural product is made from the fossilized remains of tiny freshwater organisms. Its granular texture has the effect of scraping the undersides of the bugs crawling over it so that they end up dying of dehydration. It is completely safe for pets in the garden, but be sure to use "food-grade" DE only. This is most effective in gardens that do not use sprinklers since wet DE does not work as intended.

- Push a cardboard toilet paper roll over a seedling and into the ground, and you've created a barrier for cutworms. When the plant is more mature you can just tear the barrier away.
- Slugs and snails love a good beer. Put a shallow pan of it in the garden at the end of the day and in the morning you'll find out exactly how many came for the party and never left.

- Earwigs, on the other hand, like a good roll—the cardboard or newspaper kind. Place a paper towel roll or rolled-up newspaper in the bed and the next day you'll find that earwigs used it as a tent all night. You can just pick up the loaded tube and dump it in the trash.

Pesticides Derived from Plants

Next up on the weapons list are pesticides created from plants. While these plant-derived controls may sound "natural," that doesn't mean that they are harmless and care should be used in their application.

The safest of the plant-derived pesticides is Neem, an oil derived from the seeds of the Neem tree. Neem is an effective control for many kinds of pests, including aphids, mites, and nematodes. It is safe for animals and humans and many beneficial insects aren't harmed by it. Neem doesn't directly kill the insects; instead it disrupts their behavior, affects their growth, or even paralyzes them so they can't reproduce.

Pyrethrins are insecticides derived from the flowers and seeds of the chrysanthemum that target the nervous systems of insects, causing them to die. Pyrethrins are toxic for humans, pets, and fish, and care should be used when applying them. Rotenone is another naturally derived control that comes from the roots and stems of certain tropical plants such as the jicama vine. It effectively kills all kinds of beetles and was thought to be safe for humans, but recently there has been some question that its use may be linked to the development of Parkinson's disease. Personally, I would not use either of these last two products.

Before using any of these pesticides, please read the instructions carefully, especially the fine print about the precautions you need to take when applying them.

Chemical Controls

With the poisonous legacy of DDT and other chemical pesticides lurking in the background, it is easy to assume that every chemical control is a nightmare of unintended consequences. But it's not that simple. It seems odd, but some synthetic controls are actually less toxic than some of the naturally derived pesticides. And then there are other chemical controls that are widely used that I won't go anywhere near.

Horticultural oils are synthetic, but most of them are generally considered acceptable for organic gardening. The oils, which may be petroleum- or vegetable-based, are sprayed onto plants and coat the insects, effectively smothering them. Different types of oils are used at different times—dormant oils are sprayed during a plant's dormant period and summer oils are used in summertime.

Insecticidal soaps are made from potassium fatty acids and are effective against soft-bodied insects like aphids, mites, whiteflies, and mealybugs. The soap works by disrupting cell membranes in the insects, causing them to die, but it leaves most beneficial insects unharmed. It can be toxic for some plants, however, and you may want to test a few leaves to see how the plant reacts before applying more broadly. A 2% solution is what is usually recommended, but the solution can be made stronger or weaker as desired.

Insecticidal soap is also an effective control for powdery mildew, but generally needs repeated applications.

Beyond these controls, however, things get more serious. Neonicotinoids, a synthetic version of nicotine, have been used extensively in agriculture and have been considered safe, but there is now concern that they may have played a role in the colony collapse disorder that has decimated so many bee colonies in recent years. Pyrethroids are synthetic versions of pyrethrins and are toxic to fish and other aquatic life, so there is great concern about contaminated runoff getting into water systems. Carbaryl, also sold under the name Sevin, is effective and widely used on food crops in the United States, but it kills insects indiscriminately—beneficials as well as pests. It's also classified as a likely human carcinogen, which I translate to mean "it's not worth it."

As with the plant-derived pesticides, do not apply any of these controls without reading all of the instructions for application and taking the appropriate precautions.

Bacterial Controls

One popular pesticide that is a microbial control is *Bacillus thuringiensis*, or B.t. It is very effective against caterpillars and worms; when they eat the leaves of a plant sprayed with B.t., they become infected with the bacterium and die. The problem is it kills *any* caterpillar, including those of butterflies and moths that are not pests. For that reason, it should be applied very specifically and not sprayed in any general way around your garden.

Common Insect Pests

A number of insects become damaging pests on vegetables and fruits, but they mostly fall into two categories: sucking insects and chewing insects. Sucking insects don't often kill a plant unless they attack a very young seedling. But by sucking moisture and nutrients out of tender plant tissues, they can really inhibit a plant's ability to thrive. One thing you will note about many sucking insects is that they are often in the company of a pretty serious ant infestation. That's because ants use insects such as aphids and scale to get the honeydew that these insects secrete. If you can control the ant population, you can more easily control the sucking insects in your garden.

While sucking insects can rob a plant of its vigor, some chewing insects, on the other hand, can decimate a plant in pretty short order. These insects, which include many kinds of beetles, cutworms, earwigs, and caterpillars, can be voracious and chew a plant right down to the stem, or in the case of cutworms, saw it off at ground level. It's important to note, however, that some of the most damaging chewing insects, caterpillars, will turn into butterflies and moths that will act as pollinators, so in some cases you may want to pick your battles and allow a certain amount of feeding by some insects.

The following insects are some of the most common pests you're likely to find in your garden:

1. **Aphids:** These soft-bodied insects can be as small as the head of a pin or as large as the head of a match and appear black, white, pink, or light green. You'll usually see them clustered around the newest, most tender leaves and buds. In addition to the damage they do by sucking, the honeydew they secrete can lead to the development of sooty mold.

2. **Beetles:** There are various types of common beetles, from cucumber beetles, which can have striped bodies or spotted bodies similar to ladybugs. In addition to the chewing damage done by the adult beetles, the beetle larvae can damage roots as well.

3. **Cutworms:** These short white or light brown larvae will wrap around the stem of a plant at ground level and chew it completely off. Some cutworms will crawl up onto the plants to feed on the buds, leaves, and fruit. They mostly stay underground during the day; you may find them in the soil, curled into a C shape.

4. **Mealybugs:** These tiny multi-legged insects look like they are covered with a fine coating of cotton. Like aphids, they suck on tender growth and secrete honeydew that can lead to sooty mold. They can often be a problem for citrus trees.

5. **Mites:** These tiny pests will often target plants that are stressed by drought. You may notice weblike material across leaves or yellow stippling on leaves. If you suspect mites may be the problem, hold a piece of white paper below the affected foliage and tap the leaves. They will appear as black specks falling onto the paper.

6. **Scales:** To the naked eye, scales appear as small brown, black, or light-colored bumps on stems or leaves. Their sucking leaves behind yellow marks on the foliage and can seriously stunt a plant. Scales can be harder to remove than aphids with a blast of water from a hose and may require the use of horticultural oil or insecticidal soap.

Pests Chart

Plant	Insect	Control
Almond	Spider mites	Blast with water; yellow sticky traps
	Squirrels and birds	Netting
Apple	Codling moth	Pheromone traps
	Apple maggot flies	Trichogramma wasps
	Woolly apple aphids	Horticultural oil
	San Jose scale	
Apricot	Nematodes	Choose apricots grafted on Manchurian rootstock
Artichoke	Aphids	Neem oil
	Earwigs	Diatomaceous earth
	Snails and slugs	
Asparagus	Asparagus beetles	Handpick or spray with water; use row covers
	Gophers	Line trenches with hardware cloth
Avocado	Persea mite	Predatory mites
	Squirrels and rats	Tin trunk wraps
Banana	Scales	Control ants; Neem oil
	Aphids	
Basil	Snails and slugs	Diatomaceous earth

Plant	Insect	Control
Bean	Aphids	Blast with water
	Cucumber and other beetles	Handpick; row covers
	Spider mites	Yellow sticky traps
	Whiteflies	
Beet	Aphids	Blast with water
	Cutworms	Paper collars around plants
	Flea beetles	Row Covers
	Leaf miners	
Blueberry	Birds	Netting
Brambleberry	Birds	Netting
Broccoli	Cabbage root flies	B.t.
	Cabbageworms	
	Flea beetles	Row covers
	Cabbage loopers	
Brussels sprouts	Cabbageworms	B.t.
	Cabbage loopers	Row covers
Cabbage	Cabbageworms	B.t.
	Cabbage loopers	Row covers
	Aphids	Blast with water
	Cutworms	Paper collars around plants
Carrot	Carrot fly maggots	Row covers
	Rodents	
Cauliflower	Cabbageworms	B.t.
	Cabbage loopers	Row covers
	Aphids	Blast with water
	Cutworms	Paper collars around plants
Celery	None of note	
Cherry	Birds	Netting
	Cherry fruit fly maggots	Horticultural oil
	Tent caterpillars	Keep area clear of debris and fruit
	Aphids	Blast with water; Neem oil
Cilantro	Aphids	Blast with water
	Whiteflies	Yellow sticky traps

(continued)

Plant	Insect	Control
Citrus	Asian citrus psyllid	Plant-certified pest-free trees
	Aphids	Control ants to control sucking insects; blast with water; Neem oil
	Scales	
	Mealybugs	
Corn	Corn earworm	Mineral oil
	Thrips	Horticultural oil
	Leafminers	
	Armyworms	
	Birds	Netting
Cucumber	Cucumber beetles	Handpick and use row covers
	Flea beetles	
	Snails and slugs	Diatomaceous earth
	Whiteflies	Yellow sticky traps
Eggplant	Flea beetles	Handpick and use row covers
	Spider mites	Yellow sticky traps
	Whiteflies	
Fig	Gophers	Plant in large wire baskets to prevent gophers from chewing the roots
Garlic	Onion thrips	Destroy damaged plants
	Onion maggot flies	Rotate crops
Grape	Grape berry moth larvae	B.t.
	Grape leafhoppers	Insecticidal soap
	Grape mealybugs	Horticultural oil
	Birds	Netting
Guava	Mealybugs	Horticultural oil; insecticidal soap; control ants
	Scales	
	Whiteflies	Yellow sticky traps
Kale	None of note	
Kiwi	Cats	Provide a barrier around the trunk to keep cats away
	Root knot nematodes	Beneficial nematodes
Kohlrabi	None of note	

Plant	Insect	Control
Leek	None of note	
Lettuce	Whiteflies	Sticky traps
	Snails and slugs	Diatomaceous earth
	Earwigs	
Loquat	Scale	Insecticidal soap
	Fruit flies	
	Birds	Netting
	Deer	Fencing
Melon	Cucumber beetles	Handpick and use row covers
	Flea beetles	
	Snails and slugs	
	Whiteflies	Yellow sticky traps
Okra	Aphids	Insecticidal soap
	Whiteflies	Sticky traps
	Root knot nematode	Clean debris; rotate crops
Olive	Olive fruit flies	Clean up debris
Onion	Thrips	Destroy damaged plants
	Onion root maggots	Rotate crops
Parsley	Anise swallowtail butterfly larvae	Handpick
Parsnip	Carrot fly maggots	Row covers
	Rodents	
Passion fruit	Snails and slugs	Handpick; diatomaceous earth
	Nematodes	Choose yellow passion fruit or hybrids grafted on yellow passion fruit rootstock
Pea	Pea weevils	Horticultural oil, insecticidal soap, or pyrethrins
	Aphids	
	Thrips	
Peach	Peach tree borers	Contact Cooperative Extension Office for information on treating
	San Jose scale	Horticultural oil with lime sulfur
	Plum curculio	During blossom period, shake trees to dislodge insects; clean up debris and fallen fruit

(continued)

Plant	Insect	Control
Pear	Codling moths Scales	Spray horticultural oil in dormant season; clean up debris
	Pear psylla Scab	Plant resistant varieties
Pecan	Weevils Shuckworms	Collect nuts off the ground immediately before bugs can get in
	Webworms	B.t.
	Aphids Scales	Control ants; Neem oil
Pepper	Aphids	Insecticidal soap
	Whiteflies	Sticky traps
	Cutworms	Paper collars
	Pepper weevils	Destroy infested plants after harvest
Persimmon	Mealybugs Scales	Insecticidal soap; control ants
	Whiteflies Thrips	Yellow sticky traps
Pineapple guava	Scales	Blast with water; Neem oil
Plum	Peach tree borers	Contact Cooperative Extension Office for information on treating
	Aphids Scales	Horticultural oil with lime sulfur
Pomegranate	Scales	Horticultural oil
	Thrips Mites	Yellow sticky traps
Potato	Colorado potato beetles Flea beetles	Handpick and use row covers
	Aphids	Insecticidal soap
Quince	Codling moths	Pheromone traps
	Curculios	Trichogramma wasps
	Scales Borers	Horticultural oil

Plant	Insect	Control
Radish	Flea beetles	Handpick
Rhubarb	Beetles	Handpick
	Snails and slugs	Diatomaceous earth
Spinach	Leaf miners	Sticky traps
	Whiteflies	
Squash	Cucumber beetles	Handpick
	Snails and slugs	Diatomaceous earth
	Cutworms	Paper collars
Strawberry	Snails and slugs	Handpick
	Japanese beetles	
	Brown tarnish bugs	Clean up debris and rotate crops
	Aphids	Insecticidal soap
	Mites	
Sweet potato	Flea beetles	Handpick; row covers
	Cucumber beetles	
	Wireworms	Clean up debris
Swiss chard	Aphids	Insecticidal soap
	Leafminers	
	Snails and slugs	Handpick; diatomaceous earth
Thyme	None of note	
Tomato	Tomato hornworms	Handpick
	Tobacco budworms	
	Flea beetles	
	Whiteflies	Sticky traps
Turnip	Root maggots	Apply B.t.; handpick; rotate crops; use row covers
	Caterpillars	

DISEASES

Several types of diseases affect plants, but the most common are bacterial (such as fireblight or bacterial leaf spot), viral (such as mosaic virus), and fungal (such as fusarium wilt or verticillium wilt). Some diseases will devastate a plant, some will wipe out an entire crop, and the worst of them will live in the soil and infect other plants year after year. Verticillium wilt is one disease that can live in the soil for decades; once infected, the soil is suitable only for growing verticilium-resistant plants.

So this business of keeping plants healthy and disease-free is not something to be taken lightly. While some diseases, like fireblight, may be manageable, others mean sure death for the plant. So the best approach is clearly disease prevention.

The first step begins with plant selection. Choose varieties that are disease-resistant. Plants are often labeled with letter codes. Those codes indicate diseases to which the plant is resistant.

Here are some of the codes used:

Code	Disease Resistance
V	Verticillium Wilt
F	Fusarium Wilt
FF	Fusarium, races 1 and 2
FFF	Fusarium, races 1, 2, and 3
N	Nematodes*
A	Alternaria
T	Tobacco Mosaic Virus
St	Stemphylium (Gray Leaf Spot)
TSWV	Tomato Spotted Wilt Virus

* Nematodes aren't diseases but microscopic organisms in the soil that can carry disease.

That may mean being extra careful with the varieties of heirloom plants that you grow. Some heirloom vegetables and fruits fell out of favor for the simple reason that they were particularly susceptible to certain diseases. Some growers are now grafting heirloom varieties onto disease-resistant rootstocks for exactly this reason. Choosing a grafted heirloom, when available, or a hybrid bred for disease resistance may be a worthwhile extra precaution. Some heirlooms and other open-pollinated varieties that have adapted to your area are actually more resistant to the diseases of the region. The trick is to find the right ones for where you live.

The next step is to keep the plant unstressed. Make sure its water, nutrient, and sunlight needs are being met. Keep good air circulation around and through the plant by pruning and thinning. Poor air circulation can lead to the spread of fungal diseases. Control pest populations. Not only do infestations stress the plant, but insects can be disease carriers themselves.

Practice good hygiene in the garden. As in the rest of life, a healthy garden depends on cleaning up after ourselves and our plants. Don't allow fruit to rot on the tree or vine or fall to the ground to decompose. Fallen foliage as well can carry disease that then gets into the soil, so make sure it all gets raked up and cleared away.

Make sure the tools you use are clean as well, particularly your pruning tools. It's a good practice to keep disinfectant wipes or a spray disinfectant with you when pruning so you can clean your pruners and loppers each time you move on to another plant.

Lastly, don't forget to rotate crops. Planting the same plants in the same place year after year puts your soil at risk of becoming a breeding ground for diseases and pests. By moving your crops around you break the chain of susceptibility that occurs from season after season of genetically similar plants. Building up healthy, well-draining soil that's rich in organic matter is also one of the best defenses to disease—that really can't be overstated.

Common Plant Diseases

In some cases, being able to identify a disease early can mean the difference between controlling the damage on a single afflicted plant and seeing the disease spread throughout your garden. The following are some of the more common serious plant diseases and some identifying symptoms:

➤ **Anthracnose:** This fungal disease can cause tan or brownish spots on leaves, fruit, stems, or twigs, and can cause the plant to defoliate. The disease is spread by spores, which can be spread by rain or overhead watering. Some plants may be saved by pruning off the affected parts and destroying the clippings. Plants should also be treated with a fungicide.

➤ **Botrytis:** Also a fungal disease, botrytis can appear slightly different on different types of plants, but it generally looks like a mold on fruit

or foliage. Good air circulation and drip irrigation can help prevent it, but once it appears you should clip away affected areas and apply a fungicide.

➤ **Fireblight:** This bacterial disease can be spread by insects as well as water. It causes new shoots or even entire branches to turn black as though they have been scorched by fire. Prune out the affected areas, making sure to destroy the clippings, and disinfect your pruning tools afterward. Copper sprays can help control fireblight.

➤ **Fusarium wilt:** This fungal disease is one that really makes gardeners shudder because it can survive in the soil for many years, affecting whatever you plant in the infected area. The disease attacks the vascular system of a plant, causing it to wilt and die. In addition to being spread through the soil, it can be spread by contact with the dead plant tissue, so good sanitation becomes very important. Improving drainage can be another way to control or slow the spread of the disease. Once an area has become infected, however, planting resistant plant varieties is the best option.

➤ **Mildew:** Different types of mildew affect plants, but the most common are powdery mildew, which appears like a light dusting of flour on leaves, and downy mildew, which first appears as light green or yellow spots on leaves. While powdery mildew is unsightly but not usually lethal, downy mildew can be more devastating and can kill the affected plant. Mildew can be spread by wind, rain or splashing water. Downy mildew is more prevalent in humid conditions. Mildew can be controlled with fungicides but it is best controlled by planting resistant varieties.

➤ **Mosaic virus:** This viral disease is spread by aphids. The first symptom is a mottled or speckled appearance to the leaves. Once detected, the affected plant should be removed and destroyed immediately. The best method of control is to plant resistant varieties.

➤ **Rust:** The telltale signs of this fungal disease are rust-colored pustules on the undersides of the leaves that may eventually cause the leaves to turn yellow and drop off. It can be spread by overhead watering. Garlic-based fungicides can be an effective control.

➤ **Verticillium wilt:** While it may have a different pathogen than fusarium wilt, verticillium wilt has similar symptoms and effects. It too can live for many years in the soil. The best control is planting resistant varieties.

Diseases Chart

Plant	Disease	Control
Almond	Brown rot	Sulfur spray
Apple	Fireblight	Prune for good air circulation; plant disease-resistant varieties
	Powdery mildew	
	Apple scab	
	Cedar apple rust	Sulfur spray
Apricot	Eutypa dieback	Prune in summer instead of during dormancy
	Brown rot	Clear debris and fallen fruit
	Bacterial leaf spot	Copper spray
Artichoke	Botrytis	No cure—destroy affected plants
Asparagus	Asparagus rust	All-male cultivars are more resistant; plant certified disease-free roots and keep bed clear of debris
	Fusarium crown rot	
	Root rot	
	Cercospora leaf spot	
Avocado	Phytophthora root rot	Adding gypsum and mulch to soil can help suppress; plant certified disease-free trees
	Cercospora fruit spot	Neutral copper sprays
	Avocado scab	
	Anthracnose	
Banana	Sooty mold	Control ants and other insects
Basil	Fusarium wilt	Choose resistant varieties
Bean	Rust	Sulfur spray every 10 days
	Anthracnose	Choose resistant varieties
	Alternaria	
	Halo blight	
	Curly top	
Beet	Powdery mildew	Choose resistant varieties
	Phytophthora	Improve drainage
Blueberry	None of note	
Brambleberry	Anthracnose	Plant resistant varieties; keep water off foliage
	Verticilium wilt	No cure; remove and destroy plants
	Orange rust	

Plant	Disease	Control
Broccoli	Clubroot	Rotate crops
Brussels sprouts	Clubroot	Rotate crops
Cabbage	Clubroot	Rotate crops
Carrot	None of note	
Cauliflower	Clubroot	Rotate crops
Celery	None of note	
Cherry	Brown rot	Copper spray
	Blossom blight	Horticultural oil; keep area clear of debris
Cilantro	Bacterial leaf spot	Horticultural oil
Citrus	None of note	
Corn	Maize dwarf mosaic	Plant resistant varieties and rotate crops
Cucumber	Mildew	Avoid handling wet foliage
	Mosaic virus	Plant resistant varieties and rotate crops
	Bacterial wilt	
Eggplant	Mildew	Avoid handling wet foliage
	Fusarium wilt	Plant resistant varieties and rotate crops or grow in containers
Fig	Fig rust	Copper spray
Garlic	Botrytis rot (neckrot)	Good air circulation; use disease-free bulbs
	Basal rot	Destroy infected plants
	White rot	Pre-treat cloves by dipping in hot water
	Downy mildew	Good air circulation
Grape	Powdery mildew	Sulfur spray; choose resistant varieties
	Anthracnose	
	Black rot	
	Pierce's disease	Destroy infected vines
Guava	Fusarium wilt	Plant resistant varieties
	Anthracnose	
Kale	None of note	
Kiwi	Root rot	Improve drainage or plant in raised beds
Kohlrabi	None of note	

(continued)

Plant	Disease	Control
Leek	None of note	
Lettuce	None of note	
Loquat	Fireblight	Remove affected branches; copper spray
	Crown rot	Improve drainage
Melon	Mildew	Avoid getting water on foliage
	Verticillium wilt	Plant resistant varieties and rotate crops
	Fusarium wilt	
Okra	Leaf spot	Avoid getting water on foliage; prune away affected leaves; rotate crops
	Anthracnose	Plant resistant varieties; rotate crops
	Rust	
	Powdery mildew	
Olive	Olive knot	Clean pruning tools to prevent spread
	Verticillium wilt	Do not plant in infected soil
Onion	Botrytis	Use disease-free bulbs
	Downy mildew	Good air circulation
Parsley	None of note	
Parsnip	None of note	
Passion fruit	Fusarium wilt	Do not plant in infected soil
Peas	Powdery mildew	Sulfur spray
	Fusarium wilt	Plant resistant varieties; rotate crops; clean up debris
	Pea enation mosaic virus	
Peach	Peach leaf curl	Copper or lime sulfur spray; clean up debris
	Brown rot	
	Powdery mildew	
Pear	Fireblight	Remove affected branches; clean pruning tools
Pecan	Scab	Spray zinc sulfate in dormant season
Pepper	Verticillium wilt	Plant resistant varieties
	Fusarium wilt	
	Tobacco mosaic virus	

Plant	Disease	Control
Persimmon	Root rot	Improve drainage
Pineapple guava	None of note	
Plum	Brown rot	Horticultural oil with lime sulfur sprayed in dormant season
Pomegranate	Fruit heart-rot fungus	Clean up debris; spray horticultural oil in dormant season
Potato	Verticillium wilt Late blight Early blight Mosaic virus	Plant certified disease-free/ disease-resistant seed potatoes
Quince	Fireblight	Remove affected branches; clean pruning tools
Radish	None of note	
Rhubarb	Crown rot	Remove infected leaves; apply Neem or B.t.
Spinach	Downy mildew	Insecticidal soap
	Fusarium wilt	Plant resistant varieties
Squash	Mildew	Plant resistant varieties; apply insecticidal soap
Strawberry	Verticillium wilt	Choose disease-resistant plants
	Root rot Mildew	Avoid overhead watering; apply insecticidal soap
Sweet potato	Fusarium wilt Verticillium wilt	Plant resistant varieties; rotate crops
	Alternaria	Sulfur spray
Swiss chard	None of note	
Thyme	None of note	
Tomato	Fusarium wilt Verticillium wilt Alternaria Tobacco mosaic virus Tomato spotted wilt virus	Plant resistant varieties; rotate crops

(continued)

Plant	Disease	Control
Turnip	Leaf spot	Copper spray
	Downy mildew	Provide good air circulation
	Clubroot	Avoid planting in infected soil; rotate crops

How to Spray for Pests or Diseases

When fruit trees are plagued by pests or diseases, the best approach is to spray the entire plant during its dormant season. Lime-sulfur, copper, and other organic mixtures put up an excellent defense by effectively smothering fungal spores and insect eggs that can remain on the tree through the winter. Because these sprays can be damaging to foliage, it's important to spray before the leaf buds begin to appear. Follow these steps for the most effective dormant spraying:

1. Choose a day that is dry with temperatures above freezing and no rain forecast for at least the next thirty-six hours.
2. Prune out dead and damaged branches and remove any fruit or foliage that may still be on the tree.
3. Cover nearby evergreens or perennials with a tarp so the spray won't damage them.
4. Prepare the spray according to the directions on the package and put on protective eye gear and gloves. (Even though the spray may be organic, you don't want to get it on your skin or in your eyes.) Fill your pump sprayer with the mixture.
5. Begin spraying at the top and middle of the tree and move toward the outer branches. Cover the branches thoroughly so that they are dripping with the spray solution. Once the branches are covered completely, spray the entire trunk down to the ground. Let the solution dry on the tree before removing the coverings on the nearby plants.

When pests or fungal diseases attack during the growing season, you may need to spray with a horticultural oil or insecticidal soap. Like the dormant sprays, horticultural oils smother sucking insects like aphids and scale and will also work on larvae of beetles and other chewing insects. When mixed with baking soda (1 tablespoon baking soda to 1 tablespoon horticultural oil to 1 gallon water), horticultural oil can also be an effective fungicide. To spray horticultural oil, follow these steps:

1. Make sure the plant is not suffering from lack of water. If it is at all stressed or wilted, water it well and wait until it has recovered before applying the horticultural oil.
2. The best time to spray is on a dry, cloudy morning when temperatures are between 40° and 90°F. Spraying should be done when there is no forecast of rain; if the leaves get wet after spraying, the oil will be washed away and you'll need to reapply it.
3. Follow the instructions on the label for mixing the oil and water and be sure to keep shaking the container as you spray to keep the solution mixed.

4. Spray the entire plant, including the undersides of the leaves as well as the stems and branches, all the way down to the ground.
5. Check the plant again in four or five days to see if insects are still present. If they are, repeat the spraying.

Insecticidal soaps, which are potassium salts of fatty acids, kill insects by breaking down their membranes. As with horticultural oils, insecticidal soaps must make direct contact with the insect to be effective. Follow these steps to apply insecticidal soaps:

1. As with horticultural oils, insecticidal soaps should not be used on plants that are water-stressed. Water the plant well and allow time for it to recover before spraying.
2. Insecticidal soap is only effective until it dries, so it is best to spray when the spray will dry slowest. Very early in the morning or late in the day when it is cloudy or humid are the best times.
3. Spray the plant completely from top to bottom, including the undersides of leaves and all stems.
4. Repeat spraying if needed in another four to five days.

FRUITS, HERBS, NUTS & VEGETABLES

When choosing which edibles to grow in your garden, consider more things than just what you like to eat. There are the practical issues of space, sun exposure, hardiness zone, and timing. But there are other questions to ask yourself. What commercially grown fruits and vegetables are high on the contaminated foods list, carrying significant amounts of pesticides and herbicides? What fruits or vegetables have had food safety issues, such as *E. coli* or salmonella contamination? What fruits or vegetables would cost more to buy in the store than to grow at home? What fruits or vegetables have greater varieties available to home growers? What retains more nutrition or simply tastes a whole lot better when grown in your own garden? (*The answer to that last question: Almost everything!*) Here are the rules:

1) Start with a few favorites.

2) See what flourishes in your garden.

3) Try something new.

4) Enjoy your bounty!

ALMOND

Nutritionally speaking, almonds (*Prunus dulcis*) are one of nature's super-foods, loaded with vitamin E and antioxidants and linked to lowering LDL cholesterol and the risk of heart disease. Combine that with the fact that *80%* of the world's almond supply comes from California, and you've got plenty of reasons to find room for an almond tree in your garden. California's hot, dry summers are ideal for these trees, which are native to Asia Minor and North Africa, but they also need some winter chill to be productive. Almond trees are great additions to the landscape as well. My niece was married a couple years ago in an old almond orchard in Ripon, and a lovelier setting I cannot imagine.

■ When to Plant

Bare-root trees are available in nurseries starting in winter and continuing through early spring. Plant while the tree is still dormant (before leaves begin to emerge) to give it the best chance to get established.

■ Where to Plant

Almonds are best suited for Zones 5–9. They are hardy to 10°F, but require 250 to 500 chill hours. Plant in full sun in well-drained soil. Standard-sized trees are beautiful as a focal point in the landscape. Dwarf trees can be planted in large containers.

■ How to Plant

Plant in a hole twice as wide but no deeper than the rootball. Make sure soil does not cover the graft union (where the shoot and root stem/rootstock meet). Take care that roots do not dry out before planting, and water well once planted. Once it's in the ground, prune off the top third of the tree; this will encourage better root formation and a healthier tree structure.

Most standard trees require a second tree of a compatible variety for cross-pollination. If space is tight, you can plant two different varieties of standard trees in the same hole (18 to 24 inches apart) or plant a dwarf variety nearby in order to cross pollinate.

■ Care and Maintenance

Mulch each year with compost. Almonds require moderate water but are fairly drought-resistant once established. During dry summers they will require occasional deep watering. During the first three to five years, prune to an open center to allow better sun exposure and improved air circulation. Nuts grow on short wood spurs that produce for about five years. Once the tree is well established, prune each year to remove dead wood and 20% of

the old wood to encourage the growth of new spurs and keep the tree productive. You may need to cover the tree with a tight net to protect your harvest from birds and squirrels.

■ Harvesting

Nuts are ready for harvest in late summer or early fall when the outer hulls split open and the inner shells are partially dry. Shake the nuts from the tree and spread out in the sun in a single layer to dry in their hulls for one day. Remove the hulls and dry in the shell for one more week. Nuts are sufficiently dry when they rattle inside the shells when shaken. Store nuts in a cool, dry place or freeze them for longer-term storage. A mature standard tree yields 20 to 25 pounds of nuts per year.

■ Additional Information

Almonds bloom in early spring with white or light pink blossoms. Frosts occurring during or soon after bloom time can reduce the yield. If your area is prone to early spring frosts, choose a later-blooming variety, such as 'Butte', 'Mission', or 'Titan'.

Recommended dwarf varieties include 'Garden Prince' and 'All-in-One' (semidwarf). For standard trees consider the following varieties: 'Butte' (pollinate with 'All-in-One', 'Nonpareil', or 'Mission'); 'Mission' (pollinate with 'Nonpareil' or 'Hall's Hardy'); 'Ne Plus Ultra' or 'Nonpareil' (pollinate each other); or 'Titan' (pollinate with 'Hall's Hardy' or any peach (a close relative to the almond) blooming at the same time).

APPLE

Johnny Appleseed never made it to California, but it's just as well—the apple trees we grow here are so much tastier than what grew from his random seeds. Apples (*Malus domestica*) do not grow "true" from seed, meaning that the seeds that came out of that delicious 'Gala' apple you just ate will not produce fruit that tastes like a 'Gala' and may not be edible at all. To get exactly the fruit you want, you must have a tree that is grafted—new wood from your desired cultivar is cut and banded to rootstock from a hardy, though not necessarily tasty, variety until the cuts heal together and they become one tree. Apple trees sold in nurseries are all grafted in this way, and the result is that you get a strong, vigorous tree that will produce exactly the type of apple you want. You can even get multiple varieties grafted into one, giving you an apple sampler in the space of just one tree. And since commercially grown, nonorganic apples are the most contaminated produce in the markets, growing your own apples is a healthy choice—and a delicious one. I can't think of anything more satisfying than a juicy bite of a sweet-tart 'Fuji'!

■ *When to Plant*

Bare-root trees are available in nurseries in late winter, and you can usually find trees in containers through the summer. The best time to plant is while the tree is still dormant, before leaves start to appear.

■ *Where to Plant*

Apples grow in Zones 3–9, but most varieties require 900 to 1,200 hours a year at 45°F or below, so gardeners in Zones 8 and 9 should look for a low-chill variety needing only 100 to 400 hours. Plant in full sun in well-draining soil that's been amended with compost.

While standard trees grow to 20 feet tall and 20 to 25 feet wide, apples can still be a great choice for small-space gardens. They can easily be espaliered (trained to grow by pruning or tying branches) against a fence or wall. Columnar varieties offer another option, growing to 8 feet tall but only about 2 feet wide. Dwarf varieties can also be planted in large containers.

■ *How to Plant*

Plant in a hole twice as wide and the same depth as the rootball. Make sure that the graft union at the bottom of the trunk is above the soil line. Water well, making sure the water penetrates the rootball and any air pockets in the soil have been filled in. Prune off the top third of the tree to encourage better root formation and a healthier tree structure. Mulch deeply around the tree, but be careful that the mulch is kept a few inches away from the trunk.

Most varieties are at least partially self-fruitful but you will get larger yields if you plant two varieties for cross-pollination. If space is limited, consider using a high-density planting plan (see page 31) that puts two or more trees in one hole. This keeps the trees small, enables cross-pollination, and prolongs the harvest.

Care and Maintenance

In areas with dry summers, water deeply every week or two. Add a sidedressing of compost each spring and fall, but additional fertilizer isn't really necessary and overfeeding can lead to more pests. Prune each year when the tree is dormant, keeping it in an open vase shape to allow sunlight into the center and to discourage disease. Keep in mind that the lower you keep the tree pruned, the easier harvesting will be.

Fruit grows on "spurs" (2- to 3-inch shoots) on wood two years or older. Spurs usually form three to five years after planting. (Columnar trees do not have spurs; fruit grows directly from the trunk.) However, it's important not to let fruit set for the first four or five years. This allows the tree to develop a stronger trunk and branch structure, and you can prune it to the desired form. Once fruit does set, water regularly. When fruits are dime-sized, thin each cluster to just one fruit, and space them at least 4–6 inches apart. This will produce higher-quality and healthier fruit.

Harvesting

Apples ripen over a period of weeks. To harvest, pull the apple up toward the branch and twist. If the apple breaks off easily, that usually means it's ripe. Still, it's best to sample apples from different parts of the tree to test for ripeness. They should be picked before they start to become mushy.

A mature standard tree can yield up to 400 pounds of fruit. A semi-dwarf produces 160 to 200 pounds, and a dwarf variety, 50 to 60 pounds.

Additional Information

Recommended low-chill varieties include 'Adina', 'Anna', 'Dorsett Golden', 'Ein Shemer', 'Fuji', 'Mollie's Delicious', 'Pettingill', 'Pink Lady', 'Winter Banana', and 'Winter Pearmain'. Self-fruitful varieties include 'Anna', 'Cox's Orange Pippin', 'Fuji', 'Golden Delicious', 'Granny Smith', and 'Liberty'.

Now, here's the catch about apples: They have more than their share of pest and disease vulnerabilities. Diseases include apple scab, apple rust, fireblight, and powdery mildew. Apple-loving pests include codling moth, apple maggot, woolly apple aphids, apple pandemis, plum curculio, and San Jose scale. Not all of these will actually damage the apples; some just affect the appearance of the tree. But even for the more serious problems, you don't necessarily have to bring out the big pesticide guns. If you're going to douse your trees in the really nasty pesticides, you might as well just buy your apples in the store. Nontoxic or less-toxic controls include pheromone traps, trichogramma wasps, and horticultural oil.

For smaller trees, there is a simple, nontoxic strategy to prevent pests from ruining your apples. I have heard reports of people using small paper bags or nylon "footies" (the kind women slip on in shoe stores when trying on shoes) to cover each apple when they are still very small. The paper bags are stapled in place over the apple while the footies can be securely attached to the apple stem. These covers prevent codling moths and other pests from laying their larvae on the apples, and when it's time to harvest, the covers can be removed a few days ahead to allow some time for them to fully color up. The result is large, unblemished apples without a trace of toxins.

APRICOT

Delicious in any form—fresh, cooked, canned, or dried—apricots (*Prunus armeniaca*) are a nutritional powerhouse. High in vitamin A and minerals such as copper and iron, they are also high in fiber to aid digestion. Not only that—they contain lycopene, which aids in the prevention of cancer and helps lower cholesterol and the risk of heart disease. Apricot trees grow 10 to 25 feet tall and are beautiful in the landscape, with dark, almost black bark and blossoms in shades of white, pink, or red. New leaves are bronze, maturing to dark green and turning yellow in fall, providing a year-round color show.

When to Plant

Bare-root trees are available in nurseries in late winter, and you can usually find trees in containers through the summer. The best time to plant is before the tree begins to leaf out (watch for slight swelling at the leaf nodes along the branches to signal that dormancy is ending).

Where to Plant

Apricots will grow in Zones 4–9, but do best in Zones 7–9. Most varieties require at least 600 chill hours; in milder climates look for low-chill varieties. Gardeners in Zones 4–6 should plant later-blooming varieties to avoid frost damage. Plant in full sun in very well-drained soil that is rich in organic matter.

How to Plant

Plant in a hole twice as wide and the same depth as the rootball. Take care that the graft union at the bottom of the trunk is above the soil line. Water well. Prune off the top third of the tree to encourage better root formation and a healthier tree structure.

Care and Maintenance

Mulch with compost in spring and fall. Provide

occasional deep watering. Fruits grow on wood spurs (stubby side branches) that appear on one-year-old wood and are productive for three to four years. Prune annually and train into a vase shape. Summer pruning helps control height and allows you to remove branches with unproductive spurs.

■ Harvesting

When fruit reaches the size of a dime, thin to 2 inches apart for smaller varieties and 4 inches apart for larger ones. Yes, I know it hurts to lose all that fruit, but trust me—you'll be glad you did it. Thinning allows fruit to grow bigger and healthier.

Apricots ripen in early to midsummer, and the time to harvest is short. If you miss it, fruit will quickly drop and turn brown. Pick when the fruit is slightly soft but fully colored; fruit will not ripen after picking. For cooking or canning, select fruits that are still slightly firm, and use softer, fully ripe fruit for eating fresh or drying. A mature standard tree yields on average 150 to 250 pounds of fruit per year, but apricots often produce a very low-yield harvest every other year. Putting up a few jars of jam is a delicious way to stretch out those lighter harvests!

■ Additional Information

Among standard trees that are freestone and don't require a cross pollinator, recommended varieties include 'Autumn Glow' (late harvest, 800 chill hours, Zones 5–8); 'Blenheim' (early harvest, 500 chill hours, Zones 5–9, a favorite choice); 'Goldcot' (midseason harvest, 800 chill hours, Zones 4–7); 'Gold Kist' (early harvest, 300 chill hours, Zones 7–9); 'Harcot' (early harvest, 700 chill hours, Zones 4–8); 'Harglow' (late harvest, 800 chill hours, Zones 5–8); 'Katy' (early harvest, 200–300 chill hours, Zones 5–9); 'Moorpark' (midseason harvest, 600 chill hours, Zones 5–8); and 'Puget Gold' (late harvest, 600 chill hours, Zones 5–9).

For small-space gardens, consider planting the smaller, fast-growing Manchurian apricots, which can be trained to either shrub or small tree form. Manchurians will grow in Zones 4–8 but require a cross-pollinizer. Recommended varieties include 'Moongold' (early harvest), 'Scout' (midseason harvest), and 'Sungold' (late harvest).

ARTICHOKE

As a child, I thought artichoke plants were rather forbidding with their thorny-tipped petals and their propensity to attract earwigs. In the end, however, I was won over by the succulent flesh at the base of those petals and their even more delectable hearts. Now I would brave more than earwigs for a taste. Although sometimes grown as annuals, artichokes (*Cynara scolymus*) and their close relative, cardoons, are herbaceous perennials, meaning that the plants die back to the ground in the winter, but regrow from the living root crowns the following spring. With silvery green foliage and flower buds that open to lavender thistles if left unharvested, they make beautiful accent plants that grow 3 to 5 feet tall (cardoons can grow to 7 feet), and they are becoming popular choices for combined edible and ornamental landscapes. With artichokes, it is the flower buds that are edible, while with cardoons, it is the stem and roots. If you want ideas for preparing artichokes, head to Castroville in May for their annual Artichoke Festival. You'll never look at these prickly buds the same way again.

■ When to Plant

Artichokes can be planted as dormant roots in the fall for a spring harvest. Young plants can also be planted in winter or early spring.

If growing from seed, start indoors eight to twelve weeks before the last frost. Seedlings can be transplanted as soon as danger of frost has passed.

reas, plant artichokes from root divisions in the
est. In colder areas, plant roots or plants in winter

own in Zones 8–9 and are happiest in coastal climates
mers. Cardoons tolerate more extremes of heat and
w in Zones 6–11. Both require full sun, but like
ie hottest areas.

apart in mild climates or 2 feet apart in colder regions
oots just above the soil level. Mulch heavily.

ce

suckers, so water thoroughly every week. Fertilize
and after harvest. Cardoons only need feeding in the
with less water than artichokes but have tougher stalks.
ellow, cut stalks almost to the ground. In cold-winter
foot, tie them down over the root crowns, and pile
)ke plants are generally productive for about five years
aced.

Is when still tightly closed by cutting an inch or two
ud. Baby artichokes can be harvested and eaten whole
;er than an apricot. Larger buds become tougher and
petals must be peeled off and eaten individually. After removing the last bud,
cut the main stalk down to just above the ground to encourage a second
crop. Along the Central California coast, you can often get a second harvest
in the fall. To make them less bitter, cardoons must be blanched, starting
about a month before harvest, usually in the spring. Tie the leaves up
around the top and wrap the rest of the plant in burlap or newspaper. After
a month, discard the outer leaves and harvest the whitened inner leaves.

■ *Additional Information*

'Green Globe' is the favorite California artichoke, but 'Imperial Star' is also
popular. 'Violetto' is an attractive purple variety that turns green when
cooked. Cardoons are often not sold by variety, but some of the more tender
cultivars are 'Gigante', 'Gobbo di Nizzia', and 'Tenderheart'.

ASPARAGUS

I never used to like asparagus (*Asparagus officinalis*), but when a former boyfriend prepared it for me, lightly steamed with Hollandaise sauce, I learned to love it (and Hollandaise sauce!). The boyfriend is history, but my love affair with asparagus endures. Growing it requires a bit of patience, since it takes two to three years to become fully productive. But in the meanwhile you get to enjoy its beautiful, feathery foliage, lovely against a fence or at the back of a flower bed. And when you taste those first tender, delicious spears, I'm sure you'll agree that it's worth the wait. Plus, there's an additional reward for your patience: asparagus plants continue to produce for ten to fifteen years. That's a pretty big payoff for a single planting.

▥ When to Plant

Asparagus can be grown from seed, but it is more commonly grown from root crowns, which cuts a year off the waiting time for the plants to produce. Plant in fall or early winter in mild-winter climates or in early spring in colder areas.

▥ Where to Plant

Asparagus is rather hardy and can be grown in Zones 2–8 and in arid parts of Zone 9. Plant in full sun if the soil is fast draining.

▥ How to Plant

To plant root crowns, prepare a trench 1 foot wide and 8 to 10 inches deep. If you are planting in rows, space the trenches 4 to 6 feet apart. Mound loose soil that's been mixed with compost or composted manure at the bottom of the trench and soak it well with water. Lay the crowns 1 foot apart with the tops 6 to 8 inches below ground level and spread the roots out across the soil mound. Cover with 2 inches of the soil/compost mixture and water again. As the plants grow, fill in more soil and compost, a few inches at a time, making sure not to cover the tips of the plants. Stick a finger into the soil to test the moisture level and water deeply whenever it feels dry around the roots.

▥ Care and Maintenance

The first year following planting, the plants are building a root mass and there will be no harvest. In the late fall or early winter the plants will turn brown; cut the stems to the ground and clear the debris away to help control asparagus beetles. In areas with snowy winters, you can leave the stalks up until the spring to catch some of the snow and keep it away from the root crowns.

■ *Harvesting*

To harvest, cut the spears at a 45-degree angle to the soil. The second year following planting, you can cut spears for four to six weeks. After that, just let the plants grow. The third year, you can harvest for eight to ten weeks. At the end of each harvest apply additional compost or fertilizer and water deeply. By harvesting in this way, the plant is able to continue to build a healthy, substantial root mass, which will enable it to be productive for many more years.

■ *Additional Information*

Asparagus varieties fall into two categories: "traditional" or "all-male." Traditional varieties are open-pollinated and will produce male and female plants. "All-male" may still produce an occasional female plant, which you can spot by its red berries. But because the male plants don't have to put energy into producing seeds, they produce more and larger spears. The all-males are also more resistant to diseases such as rust, fusarium crown rot, and root rot.

For all-male plants, try 'Jersey Giant' (especially recommended for colder climates), 'Jersey King', and 'Jersey Knight'. For open-pollinated plants, try 'Purple Passion' or 'Viking'.

AVOCADO

Is there anything more iconic of California cuisine than an avocado? Whether sliced into a salad or sandwich, or blended into a spicy guacamole dip or topping for Mexican food, avocados (*Persea americana*) are what the rest of the world thinks we Californians live on. And why not? Avocados are not only delicious, they're loaded with that oxymoronic Holy Grail called *healthy fat*. The monosaturated oil in avocados has been shown to help lower LDL (the bad cholesterol). They're also a good source of dietary fiber, vitamin K, and folate. That's all well and good, but they're also creamy and versatile and not at all difficult to grow. They make beautiful evergreen landscape trees, providing dense shade and growing up to 40 feet tall.

When to Plant

The best time to plant a young avocado tree is March through June.

Where to Plant

Avocados grow well in Zones 9–11 in full sun and well-drained, slightly acidic (pH 6.0–6.5) soil. In cooler regions dwarf trees can be planted in containers or other situations where they can be protected from wind and frost.

How to Plant

Avocado trees are shallow rooted and the roots are somewhat delicate. Plant the tree in a hole as deep as the rootball and twice as wide. If it is at all root-bound, loosen or trim away circular roots. Fill the hole with loose soil and mulch heavily, keeping the mulch several inches away from the trunk base.

▣ Care and Maintenance

Keep the soil moist but not wet; good drainage is necessary to keep from drowning the roots. Avocados are also sensitive to excessive salts in either the soil or water, and these salts can easily build up in containers, resulting in stunted growth or browning at the leaf edges. To flush the salts, flood the container with water once a month, three or four times in an hour. Feed with a balanced fertilizer in spring and summer. Yellow leaves are a sign of chlorosis; this can be treated or prevented by adding iron and zinc chelates (chemical compound) with the fertilizer.

Avocados are large trees, so to keep harvesting manageable, prune the trees regularly to keep them small.

▣ Harvesting

It takes between six to eighteen months from the time fruit sets until it is ripe enough to harvest. Avocados should be harvested when they are mature but still hard. Cut them off the branch; don't pull. Avocados can then be ripened at room temperature until they give slightly when pressed; this can take up to two weeks.

A ten-year-old tree will yield 100–150 pounds of fruit a year, but will sometimes bear a light crop in alternate years.

▣ Additional Information

Avocados fall into three categories: Mexican, Guatemalan, and hybrids. But more important, they fall into two flowering types: A and B. Whether they are A or B flowering depends on the time of day the blossoms open and release pollen, but for best production, you should grow both an A and a B type. If space is limited, you can graft one type onto the other.

Good type A varieties include 'Hass', the most widely grown avocado in California; 'Wertz', a good choice for small gardens; 'Bacon'; 'Don Gillogly'; 'Mexicola'; and 'Gwen'. Recommended type B varieties include 'Fuerte', another popular California choice, and 'Whitsell'.

One last note about growing avocados: If you're waiting for that pit from your last avocado to grow into a tree and start bearing fruit, you're going to have a long wait. Trees grown from seed take seven to fifteen years to start producing and the fruit will likely be very different from the avocado the pit came from. Avocado trees sold in nurseries are grafted to ensure the characteristics of the desired variety carry through and are your best bet for a reliable harvest. Grafting combines the root system of a new plant with a branch from a heartily producing tree. Most avocado trees require grafting to produce fruit more efficiently.

BANANA

I've come to accept that I'll never own a private island in the South Pacific, but if I could just grow a banana in my backyard, I think I could be satisfied. With dramatic leaves growing 5 to 9 feet long and colorful flowers (which are also edible) appearing on drooping stalks, bananas (*Musa acuminata*), and their relative, plantains, are about as tropical as you can get without boarding a plane. These herbaceous perennials are fast growers, but they can't tolerate frosts and they need heat to be productive. While standard varieties can grow to 20 feet, dwarfs are best for home gardens, topping out at 7 to 15 feet.

■ When to Plant

The best time to plant bananas is March or April.

■ Where to Plant

Bananas grow in Zones 10–11. Plant them near a warm, south-facing wall to protect them from wind and frosts. Most varieties require full sun, although some prefer partial shade. They prefer slightly acidic, sandy soil (pH 5.5–6.5) amended with lots of compost. Dwarf varieties will do well in a large container.

■ How to Plant

Plant each rhizome in a 3-by-2-foot hole. If planting multiple bananas, space dwarfs 10 feet apart and standard varieties 15 feet apart.

■ Care and Maintenance

Bananas want to believe they're in the tropics even if they aren't, and that means rich soil, lots of moisture, and heavy feeding. Water regularly and mulch to keep them from drying out. Standing water will cause the roots to rot, but occasional deep watering is necessary to help flush excess salts from the soil. Fertilize monthly with a balanced fertilizer. Make sure they are protected in the winter—bananas will freeze at 28°F, although plantains are a bit hardier.

Banana plants spread by suckers and underground roots, forming clumps up to 10 feet wide if you don't control them. Only let one stalk grow the first year and in later years prune out all but one or two stalks. It takes twelve to eighteen months for a stalk to start flowering.

Scale, aphids, and sooty mold can be a problem but are best managed by controlling ants' access to the banana plant. The easiest way to do this is by applying sticky bands (brand name Tanglefoot) around the base of each stalk.

▊ *Harvesting*

Bananas form in clusters called *hands*. After fruit has set, remove the spent flowers at the end of the bunch to lighten the weight on the stalk. In late summer or early fall (approximately seventy to one hundred days after bloom), the fruit at the top of the cluster will start to turn yellow. Cut and remove the whole cluster to let them ripen inside at room temperature. If left on the tree, the fruit will split open and rot.

Each stalk will only bear fruit once. After the stalk blooms, let replacement stalks grow and then remove the stalk that has fruited after harvest. Wear old clothes when harvesting because sap from the bananas will permanently stain fabric.

In addition to using the edible flowers and fruit, you can also use the banana leaves to wrap fish and other food for grilling. The leaves perfume the food when they're heated, lending a tropical "luau" touch.

▊ *Additional Information*

Recommended dwarf varieties include 'Dwarf Cavendish', 'Dwarf Brazilian', 'Enana Gigante', 'Goldfinger', 'Ice Cream', 'Apple', 'Williams', 'Dwarf Red Jamaican', and 'Rajapuri'. Standard varieties, which grow 18–20 feet, include 'Red Jamaica', 'Lady Finger', and 'Lacatan'. The plantain called 'Orinoco' grows to 20 feet, but a dwarf version is available that stops growing at around 8 feet.

BASIL

There's not much point in growing vegetables if you're not going to grow a few herbs to season them with, and for a California kitchen garden, basil (*Ocimum basilicum*) is basic. Whether you use it for Mediterranean or Southeast Asian cooking, or just toss it in a salad to add a little zing, it imparts so much flavor that, considering how easy it is to grow, it would be a shame not to plant it. Growing to about 2 feet tall and half as wide, basil is a beautiful addition to the garden with its lush green, purple or variegated leaves and spikes of white, lavender, or pink flowers that bees love. Need one more reason? It's loaded with beta-carotene, vitamin A, vitamin K, and antioxidants. Pass the pesto!

When to Plant

Sow seeds indoors in early spring, six weeks before the last frost. Seeds germinate in seven to fourteen days. Seedlings can be planted outside after any danger of frost has passed. Sowing seeds successively every two weeks will keep production going longer and enable larger harvests for large batches of pesto and other dishes.

Where to Plant

Basil can be grown in all zones throughout California. It prefers full sun, but can tolerate partial shade. It does well in containers and also makes an attractive and fragrant foliage accent in flower beds.

How to Plant

If you grew your basil from seed, you need to harden off the seedlings before planting. This is done by taking the seedlings outside in a shaded or partly shaded area for an hour or two each day and leaving them outside for increasingly longer periods over a couple weeks. Seedlings should not stay out overnight until they are fully hardened off and there is no risk of frost.

Set hardened-off seedlings in well-drained soil 10 to 12 inches apart. Spread mulch around to discourage weeds and keep moisture in the soil. Water daily until established.

Basil can also be propagated from cuttings rooted in water. Rooted cuttings should also be hardened off before planting outside.

Care and Maintenance

Basil requires regular watering and will benefit from application of a balanced fertilizer or compost once or twice during the growing season (more often if it is in a container). Pinch out flower spikes as they appear in the summer to keep the plant lush and full. The flowers are edible, but when they are allowed to develop, the plant gets woody and stops growing new leaves.

Harvesting

The glory of harvesting basil is that the more you pick, the more it will grow. Cut branches just above a leaf node so that new leaves can sprout. If you are taking a large harvest, do it in the middle of the growing season and follow up with a feeding so that plants will be able to regenerate. Never strip the entire plant if you want it to regrow.

Basil can be dried by hanging it upside down in small bunches in a warm, dry room. You can also freeze basil in ice cube trays with water, or mix it with a couple teaspoons of olive oil, drop it onto waxed paper, and freeze.

Additional Information

There are many varieties of basil, but the most popular culinary types generally fall into the categories of Italian (or sweet), Thai, or lemon. For Italian cooking, try 'Genovese', 'Dark Opal', or 'Purple Ruffles'. For Thai food, try 'Queenette' or 'Siam Queen'. Popular lemon basils include 'Mrs. Burns' Lemon' and 'Sweet Dani'. There are also large-leaf varieties such as 'Salad Leaf' and 'Mammoth' that are excellent in salads.

BEAN

Remember those grade school days when we had to plant a bean in a cut-off milk carton and watch with amazement how it sprouted practically overnight? Well, that's how badly beans want to reproduce for you—they'll even do it on a classroom shelf under the watchful eyes of thirty third-graders. Now that you can grow them in the relative privacy of your own garden, you have several types of beans to choose from. Broad beans (*Vicia faba*) originated in the Mediterranean region and include fava beans. The other types are all from the New World and include dry beans (*Phaseolus vulgaris*), lima beans (*P. lunatus*), runner beans (*P. coccineus*), and snap beans (*P. vulgaris*). You can even have a rainbow of beans with varieties in shades of green, purple, or yellow. Aside from being nutritionally beneficial for you, beans are also good for your garden. Like other members of the legume family, beans have nitrogen-fixing nodules on their roots that not only supply nitrogen to the plant but also put nitrogen into the soil. For this reason, fava beans are often used by farmers as cover crops between seasons. But whatever types of beans you plant, by following a few simple steps you'll find it's as easy to get a generous harvest as it was to get that first bean to sprout in the milk carton.

■ When to Plant

Beans need warm soil to germinate, so there's no point in planting them too soon. Seeds planted before the soil has warmed up will eventually just rot. Wait until nighttime temperatures are consistently above 50° to 55°F to sow seeds. In most areas beans will be a summer crop, but in very hot summer areas,

beans can be grown as spring and fall crops. Fava beans can be grown as spring and fall crops, but since they require ninety days of cool weather for a good crop, they are often grown as a winter crop in really warm climates.

Where to Plant

Beans don't like transplanting, so seeds should be sown directly in the garden. Plant in full sun in well-drained soil that is rich in organic matter.

How to Plant

Soaking seeds overnight prior to planting speeds up germination. Some people recommend covering the beans with a bean inoculant powder before planting to improve the plant's ability to fix nitrogen, but I haven't found any real evidence that this is necessary. I recommend skipping it unless you have repeated crop failures. If you do use inoculant, you only need to use it for the first crop; it remains in the soil afterward.

If planting pole beans, secure the stakes, trellis, or teepee in place and sow three to six seeds 1 inch deep and a few inches away from each pole. Thin to the best three plants. For bush beans, plant seeds 6 inches apart with no more than six plants per square foot. Fava beans are very tall, upright plants; planting them as close as 18 inches apart allows them to support each other as they grow. Any bean plant can also be grown in a container.

Water daily until plants are established.

■ *Care and Maintenance*

Because of those nitrogen-fixing nodules, bean plants rarely need fertilizing. If they do appear yellow or spindly, feed with a diluted fish fertilizer solution. To discourage the spread of diseases such as rust, it is best to water at the base of the plants and water deeply—a soaker hose is a great help for this. If rust does become a problem, an application of sulfur spray every ten days will keep it under control.

Beetles, including cucumber, Japanese, Mexican bean, and flea beetles, can be a severe problem in some areas. Floating row covers can prevent them from laying eggs on the plants. If you spot beetles, which can look similar to ladybugs, pick them off by hand. If they continue to be a problem, treat with Neem oil to control adults and horticultural oil or insecticidal soap to kill the larvae.

■ *Harvesting*

For snap beans, pick pods before they become mature (when the beans inside swell up, approximately fifty to ninety days). Plants will stop producing if too many pods mature. Runner beans, which also have edible blossoms, can be picked immature like snap beans or allowed to mature until they're brown when you can shell and dry them (about fifty-five days). Dry beans and lima beans should also be harvested when they're mature (sixty-five to one hundred days). For any beans that will be dried, you can limit or stop watering when the beans start to mature in order to speed up the drying process. Once beans are shelled and completely dried, freeze them for a couple days to kill any weevil eggs, then store in airtight containers in a cool, dry place.

Fava beans should be harvested when they start to plump up, usually 120 to 150 days after germination. You can eat favas raw or cooked, with the inner skin on the bean or removed if it's tough. Fava leaves are also edible and can be eaten raw or cooked like spinach. (Note: Some people of Mediterranean descent carry an enzyme deficiency that makes them allergic to fava beans.)

Avoid harvesting beans or handling the foliage when it's wet in order to prevent spreading any disease.

■ *Additional Information*

With so many choices to try, here's a little rundown of some recommended varieties. My personal favorites are snap beans, particularly the flat, wide 'Roma' and the long, thin haricot vert.

Snap beans often can be found in both pole (10 to 15 feet) and bush (2 feet) varieties. Try 'Roma II', 'Kentucky Wonder', 'Musica', 'Blue Lake', 'Purple Queen', or 'Ramdor'.

For lima beans, try 'Christmas' or ' King of the Garden'. These are pole beans, growing 8 to 10 feet high.

For fava beans, 'Negreta', and ' Windsor' are favorite choices. These are upright plants, growing up to 6 feet high.

Runner beans are pole beans growing 10 to 15 feet tall. Popular choices include ' Painted Lady', ' Scarlet Runner' and ' White Dutch Runner'. There are also dwarf runner beans (24 to 36 inches) including 'Aztec Dwarf Runner', 'Dwarf Bees', and 'Hestia'.

Dry beans, which come in pole and bush varieties, include the ever-popular 'Pinto' and 'Red Kidney' as well as heirlooms 'Aztec Dwarf White', 'Mitla White', and 'New Mexico Appaloosa'.

BEET

I love plants that are edible in more than one way—they're like a culinary twofer. Beets (*Beta vulgaris*) are like that. You can eat both the red or gold root bulb as well as the leafy greens, making it a particularly valuable crop for a small-space garden. As a kid, I'd never tasted any kind of beet other than the pickled ones from a can, and I was never a big fan of those. When I finally discovered how delicious a fresh roasted beet was—wow! Sweet, mellow, and as satisfying as a new potato. I like the greens simply sautéed in olive oil with sea salt and crushed red pepper. And it's good to know that besides tasting great, beets are rich in antioxidants, vitamins C and A, niacin, and potassium, and they're low in calories.

■ When to Plant

Plant beets from February to June or from August to September. In mild-winter areas, beets can also be planted through the fall for a winter harvest.

■ Where to Plant

Beets can grow in all areas in California as long as they're planted in full sun in well-draining soil.

■ How to Plant

Soak seeds overnight before planting to speed up germination. Sow seeds 1 inch apart in rows 8 to 10 inches apart. Cover with ¼ inch of compost, sand, or vermiculite, and tamp down to ensure the seed makes contact with the soil. Water daily. Seeds should germinate in five to ten days. When seedlings are still small (3 to 4 inches), thin the plants to 3 to 4 inches apart. (The thinned seedlings are edible and can be added to salads.)

You can also buy beet seedlings in six-packs to transplant. Be sure to separate the individual seedlings and plant at least 4 inches apart.

To prolong the harvest, plant successive crops every two to four weeks.

■ Care and Maintenance

As the beets are growing keep the plants evenly moist. If plants start to look crowded, it may be necessary to thin them again so the roots have enough room to develop.

■ Harvesting

Beets generally mature about fifty-five days from germination. You can harvest greens when they're 5–6 inches tall. It's best to harvest the roots while they're less than 2 inches in diameter; they get tougher and woodier as they get bigger.

■ Additional Information

Red beet varieties include 'Detroit Dark Red', 'Crosby's Egyptian', 'Red Sangria', 'Baby Ball', 'Kleine Bol', 'Bull's Blood', and 'Lutz Green Leaf'. Golden beets are a beautiful orange color (and don't stain your hands as red beets do). 'Chiogga' roots have vivid rings of red and white when you cut them open but the colored rings fade when cooked. 'Cylindra' or 'Forma Nova' beets are an heirloom variety that are longer and more tubular in shape, and are noted for being exceptionally tender.

In case you're looking for one more way to enjoy beets, try this: beet chips! Wash and slice the beets in ⅛-inch slices using a mandoline. Fry them in hot (350°F) oil about three to four minutes until the edges curl and they stop bubbling. Drain on paper towels and sprinkle with salt.

BLUEBERRY

Let me count the ways that blueberries can enhance an otherwise ordinary dish. In salads, pancakes, oatmeal, muffins—no, there's just too many ways to count! Just a couple blueberry (*Vaccinium* spp.) shrubs in your garden can put 10 to 12 pints of organic antioxidant-rich berries in your family's diets every year without having to pay grocery store prices. For a larger harvest, consider planting a row of bushes as a hedge. You'll be in blueberry heaven for years to come!

■ When to Plant

In cold-winter regions, plant blueberries in early spring. In milder climates, autumn is the best time to plant.

■ Where to Plant

Blueberries will grow in Zones 3–10. Plant in full sun or partial shade in well-drained, acidic soil (pH 4.5–5.5). If your soil is not that acidic, add peat. If the drainage isn't good, create a mound of soil to plant on or build a raised bed.

■ How to Plant

When planting blueberry shrubs keep in mind that they have shallow roots. Dig a hole twice as wide but no deeper than the rootball. For bare-root blueberries, plant with the crown no more than ½ inch below the soil line.

For better pollination and a higher yield, plant at least two varieties; selecting varieties that ripen at different times will give you a longer harvest. Plant taller varieties 6 feet apart; shorter types can be set 3 feet apart.

■ Care and Maintenance

For the first few years, mulch and water are about all the care your blueberries will need. Maintain a 4-inch layer of mulch and keep plants consistently moist (at least 1 inch of water per week). You can apply compost, pine needles, or alfalfa or soy meal for an added boost of nitrogen. If there are signs of chlorosis (leaves yellowing between the veins), add chelated iron and magnesium. Blueberries fruit on new wood, so don't prune at all for the first few years. After that, prune lightly, removing some of the older branches each year. (New wood is smooth, older wood is rough and gray.) Here's the bad news: You need to strip off flowers in the first year so that the plant doesn't set fruit. All of its energy that first year needs to go into establishing itself. You'll be rewarded with better harvests in subsequent years by doing this.

Harvesting

Blueberries ripen early spring to early fall, depending on the variety. You may be tempted to start plucking them off the bush as soon as they turn blue, but you should restrain yourself for at least a week after that until the blue skins are covered with a grayish fog. That's when they're at their peak. Mature bushes should yield 5–6 pints of berries each year.

Additional Information

Northern highbush varieties are the type of blueberries you find in the grocery stores. Best suited for Zones 4–7, they grow to about 6 feet high and produce a late spring to late summer harvest. Some popular varieties are 'Bluecrop', 'Earliblue', 'Elliott', 'Spartan', and 'Tophat' (a dwarf).

Southern highbushes are good choices for Zones 7–10. They are self-fertile but benefit from cross-pollination and produce a mid- to late-spring harvest. Try 'Jubilee', 'Misty', 'O'Neal', and 'Southmoon'.

Although not as flavorful as highbush types, rabbiteye blueberries are good for Central and Southern California and mild-winter regions (Zones 7–9). They ripen from May to July. Recommended varieties include 'Bluebelle', 'Southland', and 'Tifblue'. They grow up to 10 feet high and should be planted 10 to 12 feet apart.

Hardy half-high varieties are hybrids of highbush and lowbush and are well suited for Zones 3–7. These include 'Chippewa', 'Polaris', 'St. Cloud', and 'Northcountry'. These shrubs are very compact (18 to 24 inches high), but can grow up to 4 feet wide.

BRAMBLEBERRY

"Brambleberry" (*Rubus* spp.) is a rather quaint-sounding term for the broad category of berries known generally as blackberries and raspberries. Whatever you call them, these berries are a bountiful addition to any garden, producing baskets of fruit year after year. Brambleberries are perennial plants that send up biennial canes, growing the first year and fruiting the second. Despite their names, both blackberries and raspberries can be red, black, and purple—there are even yellow and white varieties. There are also thorny and thornless varieties, but as I learned as a child picking 'Olallie' berries in my grandmother's garden, delicious, ripe berries are so worth dealing with the thorns.

When to Plant

In cold-winter regions, plant after the last hard freeze. In warmer parts of the state, plant bare-root plants in fall or shrubs in spring.

Where to Plant

Blackberries can be grown in Zones 5–9. Raspberries are generally hardier and can grow in Zones 3–10. Plant in full sun or afternoon shade in hot-summer areas. Brambleberries of all types absolutely require well-drained soil and may experience root rot in soggy soil. In areas with heavy clay soil,

it is best to plant in a raised bed. Soil should be acidic (pH 6.0–6.5) and heavily amended with organic matter.

How to Plant

Before planting, work lots of composted manure into the soil. Plant bare-root plants 1 to 2 inches below the soil line, spacing them 2 to 12 feet apart, depending on the variety. Cut off the top growth on the four or five primary canes to encourage lateral branching. Mulch heavily with compost or leaves.

Care and Maintenance

Brambleberries need 1 to 2 inches of water a week. As long as the soil has plenty of organic matter, they don't need additional fertilizer, which will only produce lusher plants, not more berries.

For blackberries and red and yellow raspberries, train the five or six best canes onto a trellis or some other support. Black and purple raspberries form clumps with arching canes and do not require additional support.

For summer-bearing plants, in the fall prune canes that bore fruit to the ground. For everbearing plants, following the fall harvest, prune off the tops of canes that bore fruit. Those canes will produce lateral branches that will bear the spring crop. After the spring harvest, prune those canes to the ground.

In areas with harsh winters, mulch the canes with a 12-inch layer of straw.

Harvesting

Harvest the berries when they are fully colored and completely ripe. Check the plants daily, because once ripe, the berries will deteriorate quickly. Large, trailing plants yield 2 pints per foot of row. Erect, shrubby plants yield about half as much.

Additional Information

There are a number of viruses that can plague brambleberries, so it's best to plant only certified virus-free plants. Red raspberries tend to be more disease-resistant (and have better flavor) than the black or yellow varieties.

Good blackberry varieties to try are 'Apache', 'Black Satin', 'Ollalie', and 'Triple Crown'. All except 'Olallie' are thornless.

For red raspberries, recommended summer-bearing varieties include 'Cascade Delight', 'Chilcotin', and 'Tulameen'. For an everbearing variety, try 'Autumn Bliss', 'Bababerry', 'Caroline', and 'Fallred'.

BROCCOLI

Ah, the green wonder! I love broccoli—it's so good for you and so easy to grow. Besides being rich in beta-carotene, vitamin C, calcium, and fiber, broccoli (*Brassica oleracea*) also has enzymes that help your body fight cancer, diabetes, heart disease, osteoporosis, and high blood pressure. It loves cooler temperatures and is happy to pick up the slack in your garden once the summer vegetables have all been harvested. As much as I enjoy broccoli, I love broccoli raab (*Brassica rapa*, a.k.a. "rapini") even more. Its tiny buds and slender stalks are delicious when cooked in the traditional way with olive oil, garlic, and crushed red pepper. By staggering successive plantings and including different broccoli and broccoli raab varieties, you can keep your household knee-deep in those delicious florets for much of the year.

■ When to Plant

As a cool-season crop, broccoli and broccoli raab can take anything except intense summer heat (which causes it to bolt) and hard freezes. In mild climates, you can plant it in late summer, fall, or winter for harvest in winter or early spring. In cold-winter areas, you can begin setting out young plants as early as one month before the last frost date.

If growing from seed, start seeds indoors six weeks before the last frost for a spring crop or in midsummer for a fall crop.

■ Where to Plant

Broccoli can be grown anywhere in the state as long as it's planted in full sun, or in partial shade in hot-summer areas.

■ How to Plant

Work compost or manure into the soil prior to planting. Plant seedlings 1½ to 2 feet apart in rows that are 3 feet apart.

Broccoli can also be direct-seeded outdoors after the last frost. Sow seeds 2 to 3 inches apart. When seedlings have developed four to six leaves, thin to 12 to 18 inches apart.

■ Care and Maintenance

Spread a 3- to 4-inch layer of mulch around the plants. Water deeply and regularly so that the plants never completely dry out. Feed with a fish fertilizer solution once after planting and again about a month later. Keep watch for any appearance of caterpillars on the plants. Pick them off and apply B.t. (*Bacillus thuringiensis*) to control an infestation. Floating row covers can also be used to prevent infestation. To help control pest and disease problems, do not plant any crops in the Brassica family (broccoli, cabbage, kale, cauliflower) in the same spot in consecutive years.

■ Harvesting

Broccoli matures in fifty to one hundred days, depending on the variety. Harvest the flower heads before the buds begin to open, cutting about 5 to 6 inches down the stalk. After you remove the central cluster of florets, the side branches will start to form smaller clusters for a later harvest. In addition to the florets, the flowers, stems and leaves are edible.

With broccoli raab, cut the shoots and leaves. You can trim as much as you want; it will resprout for additional harvesting.

■ Additional Information

Two delicious heirloom broccoli varieties are 'Calabrese' (maturing in sixty to ninety days) and 'Di Cicco' (fifty to seventy days). 'Packman', a choice hybrid, matures in fifty to fifty-five days. 'Romanesco' is another heirloom variety that is popular both for its sculptural light green heads resembling seashells and for its flavor and texture that are more similar to cauliflower than broccoli.

Two heirloom broccoli raab varieties are 'Early Fall Rapini' and 'Spring Raab'. Both mature in forty-five days.

There's also another type of broccoli called sprouting broccoli, which is frost resistant, so it can be overwintered for an early spring harvest of little purple florets. 'Purple Sprouting' is the most commonly available seed, but another recommended variety is 'Spigariello'.

BRUSSELS SPROUTS

If there were ever a love-'em-or-hate-'em vegetable, I think it must be the tiny Brussels sprouts (*Brassica oleracea* var. *gemmifera*). The sulfurous smell the sprouts emanate when they are even a tad overcooked is one reason people give them a thumbs down. I admit I'm not a huge fan of them myself, but I keep trying different recipes and I think eventually I'll find a way to love them. Like other cruciferous vegetables, there are a lot of nutritional reasons to at least give them a try. They're high in vitamins A and C as well as folic acid and dietary fiber. Brussels sprouts have a long growing season, sometimes taking as long as four months to mature, and they are rather unusual-looking plants, with large leaves coming off a tall central stem completely covered with the small sprouts resembling mini-cabbages. If you have the space (and the time to wait) you'll likely find that they'll do well in your garden.

■ When to Plant

In cold-winter regions, plant seedlings in spring for harvesting from summer through fall. In milder climates, plant in late summer or fall to harvest in winter through spring. Brussels sprouts can also be direct seeded in the garden but only when soil temperatures are over 50°F.

■ Where to Plant

Brussels sprouts can be grown throughout California. Plant in full sun in well-drained, slightly acidic, fertile soil (pH 5.5–6.5).

■ How to Plant

Plant seedlings 18 to 24 inches apart in rows 3 feet apart. Pinch off the top leaves of each plant to encourage side growth. Spread a layer of mulch around seedlings to discourage weeds and keep moisture from evaporating.

■ Care and Maintenance

Steady watering is key for Brussels sprouts; dry spells can stunt their growth and sprout production. When sprouts begin to appear, side-dress with compost or give a light application of a balanced fertilizer.

Keep watch for any appearance of caterpillars on the plants. Pick them off and apply B.t. (*Bacillus thuringiensis*) to control an infestation. Floating row covers can also be used to prevent infestation. To help control pest and disease problems, do not plant any crops in the Brassica family (broccoli, cabbage, kale, cauliflower) in the same spot in consecutive years.

■ *Harvesting*

When the leaves begin to turn yellow, that's the signal that it's time to begin harvesting (usually ninety to one hundred twenty days after planting seedlings). Sprouts should be harvested when they're 1 to 2 inches in diameter (no bigger than a golf ball). Begin picking the sprouts from the bottom of the stem and work your way up. If you want to harvest all the sprouts at one time, three to four weeks before the harvest, pinch off the crown of leaves at the top of the plant. With the leaves gone, the plant will channel all its energy into sprout growth.

You can then harvest by pulling up the entire plant. If necessary, the whole stalk with the sprouts still attached can be kept in cold storage for several weeks. The flavor of Brussels sprouts is said to improve following a frost, but they should be harvested before a hard freeze.

One plant usually yields fifty to one hundred sprouts.

■ *Additional Information*

'Jade Cross E' (eighty-eight days) is recommended for hotter regions. 'Falstaff' (one hundred twenty-five days) is purple-red with a sweet, nutty flavor. 'Blues' (seventy-five days) is compact, fast-maturing, and disease-resistant. 'Prince Marvel' (ninety days) is particularly hardy and compact with a sweet flavor. 'Sheriff' (one hunded sixty days) is recommended for mild-winter areas. Purplish red heirloom, 'Rubine' is interesting, and 'Oliver' is an early Brussels sprouts variety (ninety days).

CABBAGE

I'm sure the smell of cooked cabbage has never really endeared anyone to this easy-to-grow vegetable, but there are plenty of ways to enjoy this cool-season crop, either cooked or raw, that make it a worthwhile addition to the garden. In slaws, salads, or stir-fries, cabbage (*Brassica oleracea* var. *capitata*) is not only tasty, it is an excellent source of vitamin C, calcium, and potassium and is also high in fiber, folate, and omega-3 fatty acids. Plant a mix of quick- and slow-maturing varieties and keep a watchful eye out for pests, and you should be able to enjoy myriad cabbage dishes through spring, fall, and maybe even winter.

■ When to Plant

Start seeds indoors four to five weeks before the last frost for a late-spring crop or outdoors in midsummer for a fall crop. In low and intermediate desert areas, cabbage can be grown as a winter crop.

■ Where to Plant

Cabbage can be grown throughout California in full sun, with afternoon shade in the hottest weather. Plant in fast-draining, slightly alkaline (between 7.0 to 8.0) soil. If your soil is not alkaline enough, you can add lime or wood ash to raise the pH level.

■ How to Plant

To start indoors, sow seeds 1 inch apart and ½ inch deep. Keep evenly moist and under a good light source. Seeds should germinate in seven to ten days.

When seedlings are several inches tall, begin the hardening-off process, then plant outdoors a few inches deeper than they were in their containers and follow the spacing instructions on the seed package for that variety. Most full-sized cabbages should be spaced about 2 to 2½ feet apart. Allowing the plants to be too crowded will prevent the cabbages from growing to full size.

To start outdoors when all danger of frost has passed, sow seeds following the spacing instructions on the seed package for that variety. Thin seedlings when they are several inches tall.

To prolong the harvest, set out a few plants every week or two, or plant both early and late varieties.

■ Care and Maintenance

Lay down a 3- to 4-inch layer of mulch between the plants and keep the soil evenly moist, preferably with drip irrigation or soaker hoses. Overwatering or allowing the foliage to stay too wet can lead to fungal diseases. Feed with fish emulsion at planting and again one month later. Cabbages can tolerate light frosts, which can even improve the flavor, but should be harvested before a hard freeze.

Keep watch for any appearance of caterpillars on the plants. Pick them off and apply B.t. (*Bacillus thuringiensis*) to control an infestation. Floating row covers can also be used to prevent damage. To help control pest and disease problems, rotate crops in the Brassica family (broccoli, cabbage, kale, cauliflower) so they don't grow in the same spot in consecutive years.

■ Harvesting

Leaf cabbages can be harvested as soon as there are eight or more leaves. Cut individual outside leaves; never cut off all the leaves at once.

For head cabbages, harvest the entire heads when they are full size, but before they start to split or flower stalks start to emerge.

■ Additional Information

Cabbages can be categorized as early (maturing seven to eight weeks from transplanting), midseason (maturing in two to three months), or late season (maturing in three to four months). Recommended early varieties include 'All Seasons', 'Arrowhead', 'Early Jersey Wakefield', 'Gonzales', 'Mammoth Red Rock', 'Red Express', 'Super Red 80', and 'Winnigstadt'. Midseason choices include 'Alcosa' and 'Samantha'. The favorite late variety is 'Red Drumhead'. Chinese cabbages fall into barrel-shaped or cylindrical categories. Barrel varieties include 'Bilko', 'Blues', and 'Tenderheart'. For cylindrical cabbages, look for 'Jade Pagoda', 'Mini Kisaku', and 'Wong Bok'.

CARROT

Many people think of carrots primarily as a diet food, an unfair association if ever there was one. Sure, carrots (*Daucus carota*) are low in calories and nutritious, loaded with vitamin A, beta-carotene, and fiber. But I've found a number of ways to enjoy them that would make your average weight watcher choke: baked into cakes and muffins; roasted with butter, ginger, and brown sugar; or steamed and glazed with honey and orange zest. Growing your own carrots means you're not limited to the traditional orange varieties. These fast and easy-to-grow vegetables come in a rainbow of colors and shapes ranging from long and tapered to short and round. And they'll grow in *any* California garden—even a container garden.

■ When to Plant

In spring, begin sowing carrot seeds two weeks before the last frost date. Plant successive crops when the previous crop is up and growing (about every three weeks) until midsummer. For a fall crop, sow seeds ten to twelve weeks before the first frost date. Once they're growing, carrots can usually withstand a light frost but not a hard freeze.

■ Where to Plant

Carrots can grow in all zones in California. Plant in full sun in light-textured, well-draining soil. Be sure to work the soil well enough prior to planting so that there are no clods or stones for a depth of 12 inches. In areas with heavy clay soil, plant miniature varieties of carrots in containers.

■ How to Plant

Work compost into the soil before planting and make sure the soil is fine and loose. Rocks and clods of hard soil can cause carrots to fork and grow in misshapen forms.

Sprinkle the seeds thinly and cover with fine garden soil. Sow seeds in rows 1 foot apart or broadcast the seeds over a prepared area.

■ Care and Maintenance

When the carrot tops are 1 to 2 inches high, thin the seedlings to 1½ to 2 inches apart. After thinning, run a thin row of a balanced fertilizer down the row of carrots, about 2 inches from the seedlings. Don't be heavy-handed with the fertilizer—it will just cause too much green growth on top and misshapen roots below. Thin again in another couple weeks if they look crowded. (The thinned seedlings are edible!)

Keep the rows weeded and evenly moist. Uneven watering may cause the roots to split. Row covers will help prevent damage from pests such as carrot fly as well as rabbits, mice, and moles.

▩ Harvesting

You can begin harvesting when carrots reach finger size, usually thirty to forty days after sowing. They will reach full maturity sixty to seventy days after sowing. In mild-winter areas, you can leave the carrots in the ground and dig them up as needed, even after the green tops die.

▩ Additional Information

The key to growing carrots is to plant them only where there is enough loose soil to accommodate the roots without obstacles. For the long varieties, that means 12 inches of light, loose soil. If that's not possible, there are many half-long or miniature varieties you can grow. Although we usually think of carrots as orange, they also come in red, purple, yellow, and white; the varieties listed below are orange unless otherwise stated.

The long, tapered orange roots that we usually see in the grocery stores are called Imperator varieties. They include 'Sugarsnax 54', 'Purple Haze' (purple skin with an orange core), 'Red Samurai' (red), 'Rainbow' (a multi-color mix), and 'Deep Purple' (purple).

Nantes carrots are fast-growing cylindrical roots 6 to 7 inches long. Varieties include 'Bolero', 'Nelson', 'Napa', 'Touchon', 'Parano', and 'White Satin' (white).

Chantenay carrots are short and stocky and grow sweeter in cooler soil. Favorite varieties are 'Hercules' and 'Royal Chantenay'. Mini carrots are baby and radish-style roots, such as 'Babette' and 'Romeo'.

CAULIFLOWER

Back in the days when mothers liked to boil vegetables to mush, cauliflower (*Brassica oleracea*) was a particularly disturbing affair. I could never learn to like it, even when it was served swimming in a heavy cheese sauce. What finally brought me around to the wonder of cauliflower was the discovery of what Indian spices like turmeric, cumin, and curry can do to it. One classic recipe, Aloo Gobi, pairs cauliflower with potatoes in a dish so yummy I think it could make anyone a cauliflower fan. In other recipes, cauliflower can serve as a good potato substitute, providing a similar texture with less starch, a real bonus for those following a low-carb diet.

When to Plant

For a spring crop, start cauliflower seeds indoors six to eight weeks before the last frost date. Plant seedlings outside two weeks before the last frost. For a fall crop, sow seeds in late summer.

Where to Plant

Cauliflower grows in full sun in all zones in California, although it is easiest to grow in cool, humid regions. In hot-summer areas, plant heat-tolerant varieties or grow it to harvest in late spring/early summer or in fall.

How to Plant

Work compost or manure into the soil prior to planting. Plant seedlings 1½ to 2 feet apart in rows that are 3 feet apart.

Cauliflower can also be direct seeded outdoors after the last frost. Sow seeds 2 to 3 inches apart. When seedlings have developed four to six leaves, thin to 12 to 18 inches apart.

■ Care and Maintenance

Spread a 3- to 4-inch layer of mulch around the plants. Water deeply and regularly so that the plants never completely dry out. Feed with a fish fertilizer solution once after planting and again about a month later.

Cauliflower comes in two types: heads that must be shielded from the sun to blanch to that familiar snowy white and heads that are self blanching. The self blanching varieties have leaves that curl up over the head naturally. For the other varieties, as soon as heads appear, tie the leaves up over the heads to blanch.

Keep watch for any appearance of caterpillars on the plants. Pick them off and apply B.t. (*Bacillus thuringiensis*) to control an infestation. Floating row covers can also be used to prevent damage. To help control pest and disease problems, rotate crops in the Brassica family (broccoli, cabbage, kale, cauliflower) so they don't grow in the same spot in consecutive years.

■ Harvesting

Harvest cauliflower when the heads reach full size but before the curds begin to separate (fifty to one hundred days after transplanting, depending on the variety). Some overwintering varieties may take up to six months to mature.

■ Additional Information

Count cauliflower as yet another vegetable that is now available in a rainbow of colors. There are still many of the classic white varieties around, but you can also get heads in orange, light green, and purple as well. The orange ones are significantly higher in vitamin A than the white, and the purple ones are higher in antioxidants.

White varieties include 'All the Year Round' (self blanching, seventy to eighty days), 'Early Snowball' (heirloom, sixty to eighty-five days), 'Snow Crown' (self blanching, fifty-three days), 'Early White Hybrid' (fifty-two days), and 'Snowball' (some are self blanching, sixty-five to seventy-five days).

For the rainbow varieties, try 'Cheddar' (orange, eighty to one hundred days), 'Panther' (green, seventy-five days), and 'Graffiti' (purple, eighty days).

'Romanesco' is another heirloom variety that is popular for its sculptural light green heads resembling seashells. It is often sold as a broccoli, but its flavor and texture are more like a cauliflower.

CELERY

Like carrots, celery (*Apium graveolens* var. *dulce*) is often relegated to the role of "diet food," which is a shame given how versatile and delicious it can be. It is a staple of many cuisines, often accompanied by onions and carrots as a base for sauces and sautés called *mirepoix* by the French, *soffrito* by the Italians, or (with bell pepper substituting for the carrots) the "holy trinity" by Cajuns. Celery is a subtle but valuable flavor enhancer and a good source of dietary fiber. My favorite ways of enjoying it are in a rich cream of celery soup or good old-fashioned "ants on a log" (celery ribs stuffed with peanut butter and sprinkled with raisins).

Celeriac (*Apium graveolens rapaceum*) is a type of celery that is grown for its root. Less starchy than other root vegetables, celeriac can be eaten raw or cooked. It's great in soups, salads, and slaws.

Homegrown celery is more fully flavored than the kinds sold in the store and won't necessarily form the long ribs you're used to. But as long as you ensure it gets plenty of water and avoid growing it in times of intense heat, you'll find that celery is a worthwhile crop for your home garden.

When to Plant

Start seeds indoors in flats in early spring. In mild-winter areas, start seeds in summer for a winter harvest. Celery is slow growing and can take two to three weeks for seeds to germinate.

Where to Plant

Celery can be grown throughout California, but it does best in cooler, moister regions. Plants require six to eight hours of sun. It can tolerate some shade, but with less than a solid half-day of sun celery will get lanky.

How to Plant

Celery seeds are very fine and easiest to sow by mixing with horticultural sand or vermiculite and broadcasting onto a flat. Keep the mix moist, and when seedlings have two or three sets of leaves, either thin or transplant. Once danger of frost has passed and temperatures are around 50°F or higher, seedlings can be planted outside 6 inches apart in rows 2 feet apart. Celeriac is planted the same way, with slightly more space (6 to 8 inches) between plants.

Care and Maintenance

Regular watering is very important with celery; never let the plants dry out. Every two to three weeks, water with a liquid fertilizer or add compost; they love fertile soil. Keep the soil worked up around the base of the plants to keep them upright as they grow. To blanch the stalks, which will make the flavor less bitter, wrap the plants in heavy paper or cover them with milk cartons that have the bottoms removed (but which still allow the leaves at the top to get sunlight). There are also self-blanching varieties. Floating row covers can be used to minimize pest damage.

■ Harvesting

Celery matures one hundred five to one hundred thirty days from transplanting but can be harvested whenever the stalks are big enough to eat.

Celeriac is ready for harvest when the roots are 3 inches across or larger, usually one hundred to one hundred twenty days after transplanting. In mild-winter areas, celeriac can be overwintered in the ground.

■ Additional Information

Self-blanching varieties of celery include 'Golden Self Blanching', 'Wonderful', 'Golden Plume', 'Michigan', and 'Detroit Golden'. Green (not self-blanching) varieties include 'Utah', 'Giant Pascal', 'Summer Pascal', and 'Fordhook'. There is also a pale yellow variety called 'Giant Gilded' and red varieties called 'Rosso di Torino' and 'A Coste Piene Rosate'.

Varieties of celeriac include 'Giant Prague', 'Monarch', 'Brilliant', and 'Mentor'.

CHERRY

When I bought my house several years ago, I was anxious to fill my small garden with trees. When I found a dwarf 'Rainier' cherry tree at a nursery, I grabbed it fast, my head filled with thoughts of the delicious yellow-red cherries that command a high price at the grocery stores. I already had it planted before I got around to doing my research, when I quickly learned that my cherry tree needed a cross-pollinizer, without which I wouldn't get a single cherry. My plan now is to graft on a branch or two from a 'Bing', and that way I'll get two types of cherries on one tree. But the moral of this story is this: Know your cherry tree before you buy!

The first thing to know is that there are two types of cherries: sweet and sour. Sweet cherries (*Prunus avium*) are the kind sold in the grocery store to eat fresh or use for cooking. Sour cherries are generally used for baking, jam and jelly making, canning, freezing, drying, or winemaking.

■ When to Plant

Bare-root cherry trees are available in late winter, and trees in containers are usually available through the summer. The best time to plant is while the tree is still dormant.

■ Where to Plant

Cherries can be grown in Zones 4–10, but do best in areas with dry summers. Humidity can spread diseases, and rain will cause the fruit to split. They also require between 500 and 1,000 hours of winter chill (hours below 45°F), depending on the variety.

Plant in full sun in light, sandy, well-drained soil. Dwarf trees can be grown in large containers.

■ How to Plant

Plant in a hole twice as wide and the same depth as the rootball. Make sure that the graft union at the bottom of the trunk is above the soil line. Water well and prune off the top third of the tree to encourage better root formation and a healthier tree structure. Mulch deeply, but be careful to keep the mulch away from the trunk.

■ Care and Maintenance

Apply a 6-inch layer of compost mulch every spring. Do not overfeed; too much nitrogen can make the tree susceptible to disease and freeze damage. Cherries are shallow rooted and should be kept moist but not soggy. Sour cherries are more drought tolerant than sweet cherries.

Prune annually, preferably in summer. Sweet cherry trees should be pruned to a modified central leader, while sour cherries need an open center.

■ Harvesting

Fruit is borne on wood spurs. The spurs are long-lasting on sweet cherries and shorter-lived on sour cherries. Harvest the cherries when they are in full color and can be easily pulled off the tree. Bird netting will help you save as much of the crop as you can from the birds. Mature standard trees will yield 50 to 100 pounds of fruit.

■ Additional Information

Sour cherries grow to about 20 feet (dwarfs 8 to 12 feet) and are self-fruitful, but most sweet cherry trees (20 to 40 feet, dwarfs 8 to 15 feet) must have a compatible cross-pollinizer in order to produce fruit.

Recommended sweet cherry varieties include 'Bing' (cross with 'Black Tartarian', Zones 5–8, 700 chill hours); 'Black Tartarian' (cross with most sweet cherries, Zones 5–7, 700 chill hours); 'Craig's Crimson' (self-fruitful, semidwarf, Zones 5–10, 800 chill hours); 'Emperor Francis' (cross with 'Rainier', Zones 5–7, 700 chill hours); 'Lapins' (self-fruitful, Zones 5–9, 800 chill hours); 'Rainier' (cross with 'Bing', Zones 5–9, 700 chill hours); 'Stella' (self-fruitful, Zones 5–9, 500–600 chill hours); and 'Sweetheart' (self-fruitful, Zones 5–9, 700 chill hours).

Sour cherry varieties include 'English Morello' (Zones 4–9, 700 chill hours); 'Meteor' (dwarf, Zones 4–9, 800 chill hours); 'Montmorency' (Zones 4–7, 700 chill hours); and 'North Star' (dwarf, Zones 4–8, 800 chill hours).

CILANTRO

If you're a fan of Indian, Chinese, or Mexican food, you are already well acquainted with cilantro (*Coriandrum sativum*), that distinctive and pungent spice used in dishes as wide ranging as guacamole to curry. You may know it by its other common name, coriander. In culinary terms, "coriander" refers specifically to the seeds, which are used either whole or ground. The term "cilantro" refers to the leaves, although the stems and roots are also edible. The plant is an attractive herb with fern-like foliage and pinkish white blossoms in the summer. The herb (cilantro) and the spice (coriander) have totally different flavors.

■ When to Plant

Cilantro has a taproot that makes it a poor candidate for transplanting, so it is best direct-seeded. Sow seeds in early spring after the last frost. In low-desert areas, plant in autumn; it will then go to seed and die in late spring. Cilantro readily self-seeds, so you should only have to plant it once, but if you want an ongoing harvest, plant successive crops every two to three weeks. Intense heat will cause the plant to bolt (seed prematurely), but it can tolerate light frosts. Temperatures from 50° to 85°F are optimal.

■ Where to Plant

Cilantro grows throughout California. Plant it in full sun, or in light shade in the hottest regions. It's not terribly fussy about soil, but it prefers well-drained, slightly alkaline soil. Cilantro does well in containers.

■ How to Plant

Sow seeds 1 to 2 inches apart in rows 8 inches apart. Cover with ½ inch of soil. Keep evenly moist. Seeds will germinate in ten to twenty days.

■ Care and Maintenance

Because seeds are slow to germinate, it's important to keep weeds under control.

When seedlings are a few inches tall, thin to 3 to 4 inches apart. Keeping the plant well watered and thinned will help keep it from bolting too soon. Pinch the flower heads immediately—cilantro is extremely quick to bolt. The mature plant will grow to 1 to 1½ feet high.

Cilantro is susceptible to a number of diseases, the main ones being bacterial leaf spot and fusarium wilt. Leaf spot is seedborne but can be water-splashed onto the foliage. Drip irrigation and soaker hoses can help control the spread. Fusarium wilt is a soilborne fungus and there is no effective treatment for it.

■ Harvesting

Cilantro is a fast-growing plant and you can harvest leaves throughout its growing stage, as long as you don't completely strip it. The flavor of the leaves does not last long once picked, so they should only be used fresh. When the plants go to seed, you can collect and dry them to use in recipes calling for coriander. The roots are also used in some Thai dishes.

■ Additional Information

Cilantro isn't always sold by cultivar name, but one of the most common varieties is 'Santos'. If you live in a warmer climate, look for a slow-bolting variety such as 'Jantar' or 'Delfino' to extend the harvest period.

CITRUS

Citrus trees are one of my favorite choices for California gardens. They are evergreen, prolific, and relatively low maintenance. And they just make a garden look sunnier! People used to think of citrus as a California icon, with acres of orange groves around every corner, but in reality the sweetest citrus only does well in the hottest regions of the state. Although citrus (*Citrus* spp.) will only survive in areas where temperatures never drop below 20°F, there are still many parts of the state where you can grow some kind of citrus, if you seek out the right variety.

The general rule of thumb is that sweeter citrus types need more heat and sour types need less. But heat isn't the only factor—frost-hardiness is an issue as well. Lemons, limes, and citrons are the most frost-sensitive and also require the least heat. The most frost-hardy citrus includes satsuma mandarins, sour oranges, calamondin, and kumquats. Sweet oranges, grapefruit, mandarins, and the 'Improved Meyer' lemon fall somewhere in between on the frost-hardiness/required heat scale.

When to Plant

In climates where frosts do not occur, citrus can be planted at any time. Elsewhere, plant trees in early spring.

Where to Plant

Citrus is best suited for Zones 8–11. Best results come from planting in full sun, but they can tolerate some shade in most areas and do well with afternoon shade in the hottest regions. Lemons, kumquats, and mandarin oranges are the most shade-tolerant of citrus, but they still need heat. If your citrus seems to be getting leggy, that's an indication that it is getting too little sun and may need to be relocated. In cooler climates, trees can be given additional protection from potential frosts by planting against a south-facing wall.

Well-drained soil is essential for citrus, which have thin-skinned trunks that will rot easily if the ground stays soggy. They prefer a pH level of 6.0–

7.5 and lots of organic matter. Add compost to the soil before planting.

Dwarf citrus trees can do well in large containers and can be brought inside or to a protected area when freezes are predicted.

How to Plant

Plant in a hole twice as wide and the same depth as the rootball. Make sure the graft union at the bottom of the trunk is above the soil line. Water well, making sure the water penetrates the rootball and any air pockets in the soil have been filled in. Mulch deeply around the tree, but be careful that the mulch is kept a few inches away from the trunk to avoid crown rot. If planted in a lawn area, keep the canopy area (total surface area of the tree) underneath the tree clear of any grass.

Care and Maintenance

Citrus need consistent moisture, but overwatering, particularly in areas with poorly draining clay soil, will kill a tree. Newly planted and container-planted trees should be watered a couple times a week in summer, more during heat waves. Established trees can get by with watering every other week in summer. Allowing the soil to dry out completely between waterings can lead to the fruit splitting.

Regular feedings of a high-nitrogen fertilizer are needed for all citrus, but in areas with sandy soil, use a balanced fertilizer. If leaves turn yellow between the veins, the tree is suffering from chlorosis and requires supplemental iron, manganese, or zinc. Apply a foliar spray that contains all three minerals.

In areas with very hot summers, citrus trees are susceptible to sunburn. You can wrap the trunk in commercially sold paper trunk bands or paint the trunks with white latex paint that has been diluted with an equal part of water.

Citrus mostly needs pruning only for shaping or removing dead or crossing branches. Avoid pruning in a way that exposes the trunk to sunburn.

There is a pest that is currently of great concern to California citrus growers throughout the state that home growers should be on the lookout

for. The Asian citrus psyllid is a winged insect, similar to an aphid, that carries a disease called huanglongbing, also known as citrus greening disease. The disease is not harmful to humans but ruins the taste of citrus fruit and its juice and will eventually kill an infected tree. There is no cure for the disease, so the only way to manage it is to control the spread of the psyllid. So far, the insect has been found in Imperial, San Diego, Riverside, San Bernardino, Orange, Ventura, and Los Angeles counties; those areas are quarantined, and you should not move citrus plants out of those areas. Home growers throughout the state should inspect their citrus trees for signs of infestation; plant only California-grown, certified trees that are known to be disease and pest free; and dry citrus plant clippings for two weeks prior to putting them in recycling bins or compost piles. For pictures of the Asian citrus psyllid and more information, go to www.CaliforniaCitrusThreat.com.

■ *Harvesting*

Citrus varieties generally ripen in late fall through winter, although 'Valencia' oranges and some other varieties don't ripen until spring or summer. Lemons and limes are considered everbearing but produce the most fruit in winter and spring. The color of the fruit is not a good indicator of ripeness; you have to taste it to know for sure, and since citrus will only ripen on the tree, don't harvest without tasting one first.

■ *Additional Information*

Standard trees grow to 20 to 30 feet high. Dwarf trees grow to 5 to 10 feet. Once you determine which type of citrus is best suited to your climate, here are some of the favored varieties to select from:

➢ **Kumquats:** These tiny fruits are not a hit with everyone, but I know several people who love them. 'Nagami', 'Centennial Variegated', 'Marumi', and 'Nordman Seedless Nagami' are popular choices. Kumquat hybrids include 'Eustis' limequat and 'Indio' mandarinquat.

➢ **Limes:** 'Bearss' grows anywhere in the state where citrus can be grown. 'Key' limes can be grown in Southern California. Kaffir limes are not really true limes but are grown for the leaves, which are used to season Southeast Asian dishes.

➢ **Lemons:** The two most popular varieties are 'Improved Meyer' and 'Eureka'. There is also a 'Variegated Pink Eureka' and 'Lisbon', an alternative to 'Eureka' that is more heat- and cold-tolerant.

➢ **Grapefruit:** 'Marsh' is best in hotter regions. 'Ruby Red' will only have red flesh in the warmest areas, but can be grown in all areas where citrus can be grown. 'Oroblanco' is a cross between a grapefruit and a pomelo and will produce sweet fruit even without a lot of heat. It's the best choice for the coolest citrus-growing areas.

➢ **Sweet oranges:** Navel orange varieties include 'Washington Navel', 'Cara Cara', 'Lane Late', and 'Robertson'. 'Valencia' is the variety most commonly grown for juice.

➢ **Mandarin oranges:** 'Owari Satsuma' is a favorite seedless, but some new seedless varieties include 'Gold Nugget' and 'Tango'. If you don't mind the seeds, try 'Clementine', 'Dancy', or 'California Honey'.

CORN

You don't really appreciate how much people love corn until you start to pay attention to the lengths they will go to squeeze even a small patch of it into their garden. If there are even a few square feet of sunny ground that they can pop some seeds into, they'll do it. I've even seen rows of corn planted in the hellstrip in front of someone's house in Berkeley.

Corn (*Zea mays*) isn't hard to grow, but it really needs two things: space and heat. It needs space because it is pollinated by the wind and therefore must be planted in blocks for the wind to be able to do its thing. And it needs heat for the kernels to develop properly. If you live in a cooler climate, you may still be able to grow an early hybrid variety, but the space issue is non-negotiable. Plant a single row of corn and you'll likely end up with a single row of cornstalks—and that's all.

When most people think of growing corn, they're thinking of sweet corn— those beautiful ears of yellow or white corn you see in the supermarket. But even in the category of sweet corn, there are standard, sugar-enhanced, and supersweet varieties. These last two types are sweeter when they're picked and also maintain their sweetness longer after picking. But besides sweet corn, there is baby corn, popcorn, and ornamental corn, which may or may not be good for eating. With so many options, if you have the space, you can almost certainly find a variety that will do well for you.

■ *When to Plant*

Sow seeds two weeks after the average last frost date. To stretch out the harvest, sow seeds three or four more times at two-week intervals. Another way to prolong the harvest is to plant early, midseason, and late varieties at the same time.

■ *Where to Plant*

Corn can be grown throughout California, as long as you have at least a 4-by-4-foot bed. Plant in rich, well-drained soil in full sun.

■ *How to Plant*

Before planting, work compost into the soil. Because it is pollinated by the wind, corn should be planted in blocks of four rows or more. This best allows for a breeze to carry the pollen from the silks of one ear to the silks of another. Space the rows 3 feet apart, and sow a couple seeds 1 inch deep and 1 foot apart. Corn seeds should germinate in seven to ten days. If some of the seeds don't germinate, replace with new seeds and the seedlings should catch up quickly. When the seedlings come up, thin to the best plant every foot. Another plan is to plant in hills 3 feet apart on all sides. Sow six to seven seeds in each hill and thin to the three strongest seedlings in each. For baby corn, plant 1 inch deep, 1 to 2 inches apart, and thin to 4 inches apart.

Unless the seed packet says differently, do not plant popcorn and sweet corn or supersweet and standard sweet corn near each other; cross-pollination between these types can have negative effects on the corn.

If you have enough space, you may want to try a planting scheme called "The Three Sisters." This is a companion planting technique used by Native Americans that groups corn, pole beans, and squash together. The corn provides the pole for the beans to grow on, the beans fix nitrogen into the soil, and the squash acts as a mulch to shade out weeds. Begin by creating soil mounds 18 inches across and 5 feet apart. Plant four corn seeds in a 6-inch square in the center of each mound. When the corn seedlings reach 4 inches in height, plant four beans, each 3 inches from each corn plant. At the same time, create mounds in the rows between the corn mounds and plant three squash seeds 4 inches apart from each other in each of the new mounds. When the squash seedlings come up, thin to two plants per mound. Keep the area weeded until the squash plants fill out enough to keep the weeds down.

■ Care and Maintenance

Corn is a thirsty plant. Expect to provide at least 1½ inches of water per week. It's also a heavy feeder. Apply a high-nitrogen fertilizer when the plants are 12 to 15 inches high and again when they are 2 to 2½ feet high.

When the tassels emerge from the end of the ears, it's time to deeply water the plants, making sure the entire root zone is completely saturated. Do this again when the silks form.

Corn earworms can be a problem and will ruin the corn. To treat them, three to seven days after the silks first appear, use an eye dropper to put a couple drops of mineral oil in the tip of each ear.

You may see suckers (additional shoots that sprout from the base of the plant) develop; do not remove them.

■ Harvesting

Typically, sweet corn is ready for harvest three weeks after the silks first appear. When you see that the silks have turned dark brown, pull back the husk and squeeze a kernel with your fingernails. If you see a milky liquid squirt out, the ear is ready for harvest. If the liquid is watery, then the corn is not ripe. If the inside of the kernel is doughy, then it is overripe.

Baby corn ripens shortly after the first silks are showing, which may be only a few weeks after planting.

A 4-by-4-foot block should yield sixteen to twenty-four ears of corn.

■ Additional Information

Unless you have a long growing season, your best bet for sweet corn is an early variety, such as 'Bon Jour', a bicolor corn; 'Sugar Pearls', a white corn; and 'Casino', a yellow corn. For supersweet corn, try 'Early Xtra Sweet' or 'Butterfruit Original Early'.

Favorite popcorn varieties include 'Black', 'Gold', 'Cherokee', and 'Pennsylvania Dutch Butter Flavored'. 'Strawberry' popcorn has red kernels on short, fat ears that resemble strawberries, although the kernels are white when popped.

There are also ornamental varieties of corn with multicolored kernels. Most ornamental varieties are not intended for eating, but the following varieties are edible: 'Indian Summer', 'Bloody Butcher', 'Indian Ornamental', and 'Smoke Signals'.

CUCUMBER

I can trace my appreciation for cucumbers (*Cucumis sativum*) back to my aunt Helen, who turned me on to cucumber sandwiches as a kid. There's something about thin slices of cucumber that makes plain white bread and butter a lot more special. My aunt also canned delicious bread-and-butter pickles, which could do things to a peanut butter sandwich that still makes my mouth water. How can I not love cucumbers?

There are four general types of cukes: the long, slicing cucumbers like the ones you see in the grocery stores; small cucumbers suitable for pickling; round ones such as lemon cucumbers; and novelty varieties that need to be grown in a greenhouse and cannot be open pollinated. While vining cucumbers can run up to 6 feet in length, there are also compact, bush-type plants that top out at 24 to 36 inches high and that do well even in containers as long as they get the regular water they require. Even in a small-space garden, you can be in cucumber heaven.

■ When to Plant

Cucumber seeds require warm soil to sprout in the spring, so wait until two weeks after the average date of last frost to plant. Seeds can be started indoors, but wait until all danger of frost has passed and the soil has warmed to transplant seedlings outdoors.

■ Where to Plant

You can grow cucumbers in all zones in California. Plant in full sun, although in the hotter regions, it can tolerate partial shade.

■ How to Plant

Sow seeds in small hills of soil beneath a trellis or some other type of support. Plant three to four seeds per hill about 1 inch deep, with each hill 1 to 3 feet apart. Seeds germinate in five to ten days. Thin seedlings to two per hill.

■ Care and Maintenance

Keeping cucumbers well watered is paramount in getting good-tasting fruit. Irregular watering can lead to misshapen or bitter cukes. Laying down a layer of newspaper and mulch will help keep the ground evenly moist and will suppress weeds as well. Cucumbers also benefit from an application of fish emulsion or an all-purpose fertilizer six weeks after planting.

Be on the watch for damage from slugs, snails, cucumber beetles, and flea beetles. Whiteflies can also be a problem, although they don't usually do

significant damage and can be controlled with yellow sticky traps. Floating row covers can minimize pest damage, but be sure to remove the covers when flowers start to appear so that pollination can occur.

Harvesting

Cucumbers will be ready to harvest in summer or early fall. Cut the cucumbers from the vine (don't pull!) while they're young to keep the plant productive. If you let just one fruit grow gigantic, it will slow or halt production of the rest of the plant. A dwarf bush will yield four to six cucumbers. Vining varieties will usually yield ten to thirty fruits per plant.

Additional Information

Some of the favorite vining varieties are 'Marketmore 76', 'Orient Express', 'Slicemaster', and 'Sweet Success'. Bush varieties include 'Bush Slicer', 'Fanfare', and 'Spacemaster'.

For pickling, try 'Diamant' or 'Endeavor'. Two favorite Asian cukes are 'Suyo Long' and 'Tasty Jade'. Other specialty varieties include 'Armenian', 'Striped Armenian', and the very popular heirloom 'Lemon'.

EGGPLANT

Not only are eggplants (*Solanum melongena* var. *esculentum*) often used in cuisines throughout Asia and the Mediterranean, they're awfully pretty in the garden. They have delicate purple flowers and glossy purple, lavender, or white fruit that can be fat and egg-shaped, long and slender, or round as a softball. The plants are fairly compact, some 2 to 3 feet wide and high, and they do well in containers, making them a great choice for small-space or balcony gardens. They are heat lovers but can be accommodated in almost any garden if the timing is right. And, oh, the things you can do with eggplant! From ratatouille to parmigiana to moussaka to baba ghanoush, the eggplant possibilities will take you around the world and back again.

■ *When to Plant*

Start seeds indoors four to six weeks before the last frost. Seeds germinate in ten to twenty-one days. Seedlings can be transplanted (after hardening off) three weeks after the last frost or when nighttime temperatures are consistently above 55°F. Eggplants require two to three months of warm days and nights at temperatures of 65°F and above. In warmer climates, a second crop can be planted in midsummer for a fall harvest.

■ *Where to Plant*

Eggplants can be grown throughout California. Plant in full sun in well-drained soil that has been amended with compost.

■ *How to Plant*

Plant seeds ¼ inch deep and at least 1 inch

apart. When seedlings are 2 to 3 inches tall, thin or transplant to individual pots. Seedlings need temperatures between 70° to 75°F and a good light source while indoors. When temperatures outside are warm enough, transplant seedlings 2 to 3 feet apart. Varieties that develop large fruits should have their main stem staked for support. Apply a layer of mulch around the plants to keep moisture in and suppress weeds.

Care and Maintenance

Eggplants need a regular, moderate amount of water and should never be allowed to dry out. When plants begin to flower, apply a balanced fertilizer.

Watch out for flea beetles, spider mites, and whiteflies on the plant. Eggplants are also susceptible to powdery mildew and fusarium wilt. Mildew can be controlled with Neem oil. Fusarium wilt is a soilborne fungus that cannot be treated. Affected plants should be removed and destroyed (do not compost!).

Harvesting

Eggplants are ready for harvest in the summer when the fruit is fully colored and before the skin loses its shine. Cut the fruit off the plant; don't pull. The more you harvest, the more the plant will continue to produce. Most of the larger eggplant varieties will yield six to eight fruit per plant. The smaller fruit varieties will yield considerably more.

Additional Information

Most of the Italian eggplant varieties do exceptionally well in warmer regions. These include 'Listada de Gandia' (ninety days), 'Nadia' (eighty days), 'Beatrice' (eighty days), and 'Rosa Bianca' (eighty days).

In cooler climates, look for the varieties that mature in sixty-five days or less, such as 'Dusky' (fifty-six days), 'Fairy Tale' (fifty-five days), 'Ichiban' (sixty-one days), 'Neon' (sixty-five days), and 'Orient Express' (fifty-eight days).

FIG

I don't know how I got by without them for so long, but it's only been in recent years that I've discovered how delicious fresh figs (*Ficus carica*) are and what a great addition fig trees are to the garden. My 'Brown Turkey' grows in a large wine barrel container in the middle of my patio, bringing a little touch of the Mediterranean to my small garden. I look forward to every succulent fruit it bears. Planting the appropriate variety for your region is key, for while figs are highly adaptable in some ways, heat is all-important.

When to Plant

Trees are available in nurseries in bare-root form in early spring and in containers through the summer. Trees can be planted anytime when they can receive adequate regular water until established. Although drought-tolerant later, newly planted figs will experience stunted growth when they lack sufficient water.

Where to Plant

Figs are well suited to growing in Zones 8–11 in California. Plant in full sun. They require heat for the fruit to develop adequate sweetness, and they have a winter chill requirement of less than 300 hours. When considering where to plant, keep in mind that figs are plants that want to grow big, with some varieties growing to 50 feet. That being said, they do well in containers and can be kept very limited in size, even espaliered, with diligent pruning, which may limit fruit production. They have extensive root systems that can run well beyond the tree canopy.

How to Plant

Plant in a hole twice as wide and the same depth as the rootball. Water well, making sure the water penetrates the rootball and any air pockets in the soil have been filled in. Mulch deeply around the tree, but be careful that the mulch is kept a few inches away from the trunk to avoid crown rot.

Care and Maintenance

Although they require weekly watering when young, established trees are very drought-tolerant. In hot, dry regions, however, fruit quality will improve with deep watering every couple of weeks. Fertilizing is usually only necessary for container-planted figs. For other figs, organic mulch will provide enough nutrients. Trees need only light pruning for fruit production. Mature trees should be pruned to control size and shape. Prune after the main harvest; if the tree bears in fall, prune only half the branches in summer and the other half the following summer. Avoid winter pruning. If you do severe pruning, you may need to use a latex whitewash on the trunk and branches to prevent sunburn.

Harvesting

Most figs bear two crops a year. The first, called the breba crop, grows on the previous year's wood in the spring. The second crop in the fall grows on new growth and is the heavier of the two crops.

Figs will ripen only while they're still on the tree. When ripe, the fig will be slightly soft to the touch and bend slightly at the stem end, and it can then be easily pulled off the tree. Fresh figs will be good for only two to three days after harvesting, but many varieties are good for drying.

Additional Information

For Southern California gardens, recommended varieties include 'Black Mission' and 'Brown Turkey'. For coastal regions, try 'Desert King', 'Flanders', and 'Tena'. Northern California gardeners would be better going with 'Genoa' or 'Osborn's Prolific'. 'Black Mission' and 'Excel' will do well anywhere in the fig-growing zones in California.

GARLIC

It may be nothing more than a "stinking rose" to some, but to much of the world, garlic (*Allium sativum*) is a basic culinary ingredient. It is essential for Mediterranean, Asian, and Middle Eastern cooking and has tremendous health benefits as well. Rich in minerals such as potassium, iron, calcium, magnesium, manganese, zinc, and selenium, garlic is considered to be heart-healthy and has long been used in traditional Indian and Chinese medicine. And it couldn't be easier to grow. Basically, you stick a clove in the ground, water, and wait.

Garlic is divided into two categories: hardneck and softneck. Hardneck is usually grown in cooler climates and includes Rocambole, Porcelain, and Purple Stripe. Softneck garlic grows in warmer areas and includes Artichoke (the kind most commonly sold in grocery stores), Silverskin, and Creole. Each of those varieties has subvarieties as well.

When to Plant

In mild-winter regions, plant garlic in the fall to harvest early the following summer. In colder areas, plant in early spring for a fall harvest.

Where to Plant

Garlic grows well throughout California. It appreciates full sun and well-draining soil rich in organic matter, but it's not very particular about pH.

Garlic can be grown mixed into flower beds and containers. It appears to repel aphids and has natural antifungal and antibiotic properties that are said to make it a good companion plant for fruit trees, lettuces, cabbages, beets, tomatoes, and more. It appears to sometimes stunt the growth of beans and peas so should not be grown near those plants.

How to Plant

Break bulbs into individual cloves and plant only the largest ones. Plant them with the pointed end facing up 1 inch deep and 3 to 6 inches apart in rows 15 inches apart. The large fist-sized bulbs called giant or elephant garlic should be planted the same way, but spaced 8 to 12 inches apart.

Care and Maintenance

Garlic is about as low-maintenance as an edible plant can get. Regular watering and mulching can help keep the moisture level even. Too little water can cause bulbs to be undersize, and too much water can cause other problems, including split skins, mold, and garlic that is hard to cure.

Harvesting

Softneck garlic is ready to harvest when the leafy tops fall over and start to turn yellow. Hardneck garlic is ready when the flower stalks (scapes) straighten up. Don't try to pull the bulbs up; use a garden fork to lift them. Shake off the excess dirt, cut off most of the leaf tops and the roots, and allow the bulbs to air dry for about a week. Store the bulbs in a cool, dark place with good air circulation. Softneck garlic will last longer than hardneck in storage, so eat the hardneck first!

Additional Information

In addition to the garlic bulbs, you can also eat garlic scapes—the flower stalks that emerge from hardneck garlic bulbs. Whether you eat them or not, the scapes should be removed so that the plant's energy can be directed into the bulb growth and not wasted on the flowers. When the scapes are removed just after emergence, they are tender enough to eat raw. You can toss them into salads or slice them and toss onto potatoes and other foods the same way you would use chopped scallions or chives. Once the scapes grow a bit more they get firmer and can be used in sautés and stir-fries. Hardneck Rocambole garlics are the ones that produce scapes. These include 'Carpathian', 'German Red', and 'Spanish Roja'.

GRAPE

I think there are two kinds of people in California—those who grow grapes and those who wish they grew grapes. I don't know many Californians who don't harbor secret dreams of someday being able to look out their window onto a beautiful vineyard. But even if you can't have a vineyard, you can grow grapes (*Vitis vinifera*).

■ *When to Plant*

Plant bare-root vines in winter in regions where the winters are mild. In cold-winter regions, plant bare-root vines three weeks before the last expected frost date. Container-grown vines can sometimes be found in nurseries and can be planted throughout the year.

■ *Where to Plant*

Grapes are grown in Zones 4–10, but do especially well in hot-summer climates. In colder regions, planting the vines against a south-facing wall can help make up for the lack of heat. Plant in full sun in deep, well-drained soil. Rich soil will make all the difference in the quality of the fruit.

■ *How to Plant*

Before planting bare-root vines, trim the roots back to just 6 inches. Plant the vines up to the soil line on the vine, spreading out the roots in all directions. Space the vines 8 to 10 feet apart. If planting near a support structure such as a pergola, fence, or arbor, leave 1½ feet between the structure and the vine and set the vine at a 45-degree angle leaning toward the support structure. Once planted, cut back the top growth to leave just two or three buds.

■ *Care and Maintenance*

Water and weed regularly. Drip irrigation is best so that wet foliage doesn't encourage mildew and fungal diseases. In cold-winter areas, stop watering after August. Apply a balanced fertilizer each spring.

Pruning is very important with grapes, both because they need good air circulation and because they bear fruit on the current year's growth. Vines should not be pruned until the third winter, and then you need to decide which pruning technique to use—spur pruning or cane pruning.

Spur pruning is the easier technique and the more commonly used technique for home growers. With this method, you simply cut all the canes down to spurs with two or three buds each. With cane pruning, you select two strong canes thicker than a pencil (but less than three times as thick) and remove all the other canes. Tie one cane going in one direction and the

other cane going in the other direction. The advantage to this method is that it provides frost protection and allows more even production and space for shoots.

Grapes can be targeted by grape leafhoppers, grape mealybugs, grape berry moths, and Japanese beetles, as well as birds and deer, but diseases such as anthracnose, black rot, and mildew are an even bigger worry. Pierce's disease, which is spread by the sharpshooter insect and can cause vines to wilt and die, has become a serious problem in California. Buying disease-resistant vines is your best bet, and American, muscadine, and hybrid grapes are the most disease-resistant.

Harvesting

When the bunches of grapes are fully colored and sweet, it's time to harvest. At the peak of ripeness the individual grapes should be easy to pull off and seeds should be brown. Grapes will not ripen further once they're off the vine. Cut the bunches from the vine with sharp, clean pruners.

Additional Information

There are four main types of grapes: American, European, muscadine, and hybrids. Except for muscadines, most grapes are self-fruitful. Check before buying to see if the variety needs a cross-pollinizer. Recommended American varieties include 'America', 'Champanel', 'Concord', 'Price', and 'Swenson Red'. For European grapes, try 'Black Monukka', 'Delight', 'Flame', and 'Olivette Blanche'. 'Cowart', 'Regale', and 'Sterling' are some good muscadine varieties. Recommended hybrids are 'Baco Noir', 'Foch Grape', and 'Missouri Riesling'.

GUAVA

For those craving a bit of the tropics, planting a guava tree (*Psidium guajava*) may be just the ticket. These evergreen trees are attractive in the landscape, and the fruit is highly nutritious, loaded with fiber, vitamins A and C, folic acid, and antioxidants. The tree is widely adaptable with one caveat—it can't handle frost. As long as you can protect it from frost you can keep your little bit of the tropics handy at all times.

When to Plant

Because of its sensitivity to frosts, the best time to plant a guava tree is after the danger of frost has passed in the spring.

Where to Plant

You can grow guavas in Zones 9–11. Plant in full sun or partial shade. Guavas prefer rich, well-drained soil, but can adapt to a wide range of soil types as long as they are not high in salt. Optimum pH level is 5–7, but they can tolerate more alkaline soil. Guavas do well either in containers or in the ground.

How to Plant

Plant in a hole twice as wide but no deeper than the rootball. Take care that roots do not dry out before planting, and water well once planted. Guavas can also be grown from seed, but they will not necessarily produce fruit that is like the parent plant.

Care and Maintenance

Guava trees are drought-tolerant, but for good fruit quality, you should water regularly and mulch.

The trees can take heavy pruning, but usually it's only necessary to remove suckers and water sprouts (tall vertical shoots that aren't fruit bearing) and shape as much as you want. In colder regions it is advisable to prune to a shrub shape to give the plant better frost protection.

Guavas are heavy feeders; apply a balanced fertilizer monthly and just before a heavy pruning.

The only pests to be concerned about are mealybugs, scale, and whiteflies, but these can be controlled with horticultural oil or insecticidal soap and by controlling ants on the tree.

■ Harvesting

This fruit ripens from late summer into fall. It is 1 to 3 inches wide and is yellow-skinned with white, pink, or yellow flesh, depending on the variety. Guavas have a mildly acidic flavor and a scent that some describe as musky.

They are best picked when they're fully colored, but they can be picked green and ripened at room temperature. Some varieties are good to eat fresh, but others are best used for jelly, purée, or juice.

■ Additional Information

Guavas are self-fruitful but most will produce a heavier crop if there is another variety nearby to cross-pollinate it.

Some of the recommended varieties include 'Mexican Cream', 'Tropical Pink', 'Tropical Yellow', 'Red Malaysian', 'Ruby X', and 'Sweet White Indonesian'.

Related to the common guava, the strawberry guava (*P. cattleianum*) is hardier and may be better suited to the colder regions where the common guava can't thrive. In California, strawberry guavas are usually grown as shrubs or multitrunked trees. The fruit is dark red to black with white flesh and has a sweet-tart flavor.

KALE

In the categories of nutritional value, ease of growing, and culinary versatility, kale (*Brassica oleracea* var. *acephala*) gets high marks across the board. It is high in vitamins A and C, calcium, and fiber; is delicious used in salads, slaws, and stir-fries; and not only tolerates frosts and snow but actually gets sweeter-tasting.

However, should you tire of all the healthy and delicious soups, stews, pasta dishes, and so forth that you can cook with kale, here's one more use you may not have considered: kale chips! Just tear washed and dried kale leaves into pieces, place in a bowl, sprinkle with a tablespoon of olive oil and a tablespoon of sherry vinegar, and mix until the leaves are completely coated. Spread out on a cookie sheet covered with parchment paper and bake at 300°F until the leaves are crisp (about thirty-five minutes). Sprinkle with sea salt and serve.

When to Plant

Plant kale in late summer for a fall harvest. In cool-summer areas, it can also be planted in early spring for a summer harvest. Avoid growing it in the hottest months because intense heat will make the leaves bitter.

Collards, a close relative of kale that is smooth-leaved and forms a loose head or no head at all, are more heat-tolerant and can be planted in early spring for a spring/summer crop or in summer for a fall/winter crop.

Where to Plant

Kale can be grown throughout California. Plant in full sun or light shade in well-draining soil rich with organic matter.

How to Plant

Kale should be direct-seeded 2 inches apart in rows 12 to 18 inches apart. Cover with ½ inch of soil, and water well. Seeds should germinate in seven to ten days. Thin seedlings to 1 to 3 feet apart, depending on the variety. Mulch with compost.

Care and Maintenance

Kale requires constant, even moisture. Apply a fish emulsion solution when seedlings emerge and again one month later. Plants will grow to 2 to 3 feet in height and may require staking.

Although pests and diseases are usually not a big problem with kale, it's still a good idea to rotate crops in the Brassica family (broccoli, cabbage, kale, cauliflower) so they don't grow in the same spot in consecutive years.

Harvesting

You can begin harvesting when there are at least six to eight leaves on the plant. Cut leaves from the outside of the plant if you want to stretch out the harvest, or cut the entire plant at once. Discard the whole plant when flower stalks emerge. Although kale is related to broccoli and cauliflower, it doesn't form a "head." It's the leaves that are harvested.

Additional Information

Kale is available in curly and non-curly varieties. Curly-leafed types include 'Dwarf Blue Curled', 'Dwarf Siberian', 'Redbor', and 'Winterbor'. Non-curly kales include 'Lacinato' (also called dinosaur kale), 'Red Russian', 'White Russian', and 'Blue-Curled Vates'. Kale that is sold as "ornamental" is also edible but should only be eaten if you know it is pesticide-free. Varieties of collards include 'Champion', 'Georgia', 'Morris Heading', and 'Vates'.

KIWI

It's hard to believe that it wasn't so many years ago that most Americans had never heard of that fuzzy, delicious fruit known as the kiwi (*Actinidia arguta*). But in the past couple decades, these Asian imports with a flavor that hints of strawberry, melon, and pineapple have become a favorite. The type seen in supermarkets is fuzzy kiwi, but there are also hardy and arctic beauty kiwis, which are hardier and sweeter and require no peeling.

Although there are a few self-fruitful varieties, most kiwis need to have a male plant near to pollinate the female (fruit-bearing) vines. One male can pollinate up to eight females.

When to Plant

The best time to plant kiwi vines is late fall or winter, just before or during their dormant period.

Where to Plant

Fuzzy kiwi can be grown in Zones 7–9. Hardy kiwi is hardy to Zone 4, and arctic beauty is hardy to Zone 3. Kiwis prefer full sun but can tolerate partial shade. In hot-summer areas, they require afternoon shade. They need slightly acidic soil (pH 5.0–6.5) with excellent drainage.

How to Plant

Kiwi vines require some kind of support structure, such as a pergola, fence, or trellis, at least 6 feet high. Have the structure in place first, then plant the vine in a hole twice as wide but no deeper than the rootball. Water well and mulch.

Care and Maintenance

Water is one of the primary care issues for kiwis—they need a lot of it and they need it regularly. They also need lots of nitrogen, preferably in the first half of the growing season. If your soil is not very acidic, a citrus and avocado fertilizer can be beneficial.

Pruning must be done in the winter when the vine is dormant. In the first year train one strong shoot up the support structure and tie the shoot to the structure. Prune out all the other shoots coming from the crown. When the shoot grows to the top of the structure, pinch out the tip to encourage lateral growth and tie the end of the shoot to the structure to keep it in place. Train two lateral branches and remove any other lateral branches coming off the main stem.

In the second year train two shoots at the top of the main stem horizontally and tie them in place. In the second winter, trim each one back to twelve to eighteen buds. The next year, clean up the vine by removing water sprouts and dead or weak wood, but be sure not to remove the fruiting spurs on the lateral branches. In subsequent years, thin the fruiting lateral branches to 6 inches apart and cut the remaining laterals to 18 inches.

■ Harvesting

Fuzzy and hardy kiwis will not start to bear fruit for three or four years, but once they begin to bear, they can produce over 100 pounds of fruit per vine. Arctic beauty kiwi will bear in about two years, but yields only about 15 pounds per vine.

You can start picking a few of the hardy and arctic kiwis in August and the fuzzy kiwis in September, and let them ripen on a windowsill or in a paper bag. Taste them when the flesh is soft. If they are not ripe, wait a few weeks then test again. Harvest all fruit before the first frost.

■ Additional Information

Fuzzy kiwi varieties include 'Elmwood' (needs 'Matua' to cross-pollinate), 'Hayward' (800 chill hours; needs a male), 'Tomuri Male' (low chill, cross-pollinate for 'Vincent'), 'Vincent' (100 chill hours, cross-pollinates with 'Tomuri Male'), 'Saanichton' (needs 'Matua' to cross-pollinate), and 'Matua' (cross-pollinates 'Elmwood', 'Hayward', and 'Saanichton').

Recommended hardy varieties include 'Ananasnaja', 'Dumbarton Oaks', 'Issai' (self-fruitful), 'Ken's Red', and 'Meyer's Cordifolia'. 'Male' will pollinate any female hardy kiwi.

For arctic beauty kiwis, try 'Frost', 'September Sun', and 'Male Kolomikta', which pollinates all-female arctic beauty kiwi vines.

KOHLRABI

Kohlrabi (*Brassica oleracea* var. *gongylodes*) is a vegetable that doesn't believe in hiding its assets. Although the leaves and stalks are also edible, the plant is grown primarily for its tasty stem, which swells up like a bulb, fully visible aboveground and easy to spot with its purple or light green skin. Its name is a combination of the German words for cabbage and turnip, but the flavor of the sweet, crunchy bulb is often described as more of a cross between an apple and a mild turnip. Popular in Asian and Eastern European cuisines, it can be eaten raw or cooked in much the same ways that potatoes are used. The leaves can be prepared the same ways that other greens are cooked. Kohlrabi is high in vitamins A and C, calcium, potassium, and fiber, and it is low in calories.

When to Plant

Sow seeds two weeks after the average last frost date. To extend the harvest, successive sowings can be done two weeks apart. In warm-winter areas, you can also plant in late fall or early winter.

Where to Plant

Kohlrabi can be grown throughout California. Plant in full sun in well-drained, slightly acidic soil.

How to Plant

Sow seeds ½ inch deep, spacing rows 1½ feet apart. Seeds should germinate in ten to fourteen days. When seedlings are a few inches high, thin to 4 to 6 inches apart.

Care and Maintenance

Keep plants evenly watered and use mulch to suppress weeds. Feed with a fish emulsion solution or a balanced fertilizer every three weeks.

Kohlrabi does not usually experience significant pest and disease problems, but keep watch for any appearance of caterpillars on the plants. Pick them off and, if there does appear to be an infestation, apply B.t. (*Bacillus thuringiensis*). Floating row covers can also be used to prevent damage. To help control pest and disease problems, rotate crops in the Brassica family (broccoli, cabbage, kale, cauliflower) so they don't grow in the same spot in consecutive years.

Harvesting

You can begin to harvest the bulbous stems of kohlrabi when they are 2 to 3 inches wide, usually fifty to sixty days from planting. Cut the stems 1 inch below the bulb. The leaves can be harvested earlier, but do not take too many leaves from any single plant or the stem will be unable to develop fully.

Additional Information

Kohlrabi comes in two colors—purple and white (actually a light green). The flesh inside the bulbous stems is always white. For purple kohlrabi, try 'Early Purple Vienna' or 'Kolibri'. White varieties include 'Early White Vienna', 'Triumph', and 'Grand Duke', which is an early maturing cultivar.

LEEK

Leeks (*Allium ampeloprasum*) are one of those ingredients that turn ordinary dishes into something really special. Potato soup? Ho-hum. But potato and leek soup? Yum! When I have leeks on hand, I'll add them to just about any savory dish I'm cooking, from eggs to pasta to stir-fries. I prefer their milder flavor to onions, and I often substitute them in recipes.

You can grow leeks very easily from seed or buy seedlings to transplant. Either way, they are a lovely addition to the garden with beautiful green or blue-green leaf tops. Those milky white stems are achieved by simply mounding dirt up to blanch them.

When to Plant

In cold-winter regions, direct-sow leek seeds in fall for harvest the following year, or set out transplants in early spring for harvest in the fall. In mild-winter regions, set out transplants in the fall. If planting from seed, sow seeds indoors eight weeks prior to planting outdoors.

Where to Plant

Leeks grow in all zones in California. In cool-summer areas, plant in full sun. In hotter areas, you can plant in partial shade. Leeks need very rich soil, so amend heavily with compost before planting.

How to Plant

Sow seeds ½ inch deep and 1 inch apart. Seeds germinate in fourteen to twenty-one days. When setting out seedlings, space them 2 to 4 inches apart in a furrow 5 inches deep. As the plants grow, mound soil up around the leeks to blanch the stems and keep the flavor mild. Keep mounding the soil up to the point just below the leaf joints.

Care and Maintenance

Leeks prefer even moisture throughout the growing season. Mulch and keep weeds pulled. Feed several times during the season with a fish emulsion solution or a balanced fertilizer. Leeks tend not to have the pest problems that are common with onions.

Harvesting

Begin harvesting when stems are ½ inch thick up to about 2 inches in thickness, about four to seven months after setting out the transplants. Use a garden fork to lift the leeks from the ground. There may be small offset bulbs that can be removed and replanted. If the leeks blossom, you may

find small bulbils in the flower clusters. Those can also be planted for another crop. In cold-winter areas, be sure to harvest the entire crop before the ground freezes, but in areas where the ground doesn't freeze, you can leave the leeks in the ground and harvest as needed through winter.

To use the leeks, slice off the roots and all of the green tops except for about 2 to 3 inches. Leeks collect a lot of dirt down in-between the leaves, so rinse completely.

■ Additional Information

Recommended varieties include 'Dawn Giant' (ninety-eight days), 'Blue Solaise' (one hundred to one hundred twenty days), 'Titan' (one hundred ten days), 'Broad London' (one hundred thirty days), 'Hannibal Organic' (seventy-five days), 'King Richard' (seventy-five days), 'Megaton' (ninety days), 'Lexton' (one hundred ten days), 'Tadorna' (one hundred days), 'Bandit' (one hundred twenty days), 'Pandora' (ninety days), and 'Lancelot' (ninety-five days).

LETTUCE

I became a fan of growing lettuce (*Lactuca* spp.) when I realized how much "lettuce" (a.k.a. money) I was spending on packaged salad greens. It soon became clear that a few packs of seeds yield much more lettuce for much less money, and by opting for the cut-and-come-again mesclun varieties, I could better avoid the unpleasant situation of finding slimy green piles of leftover lettuce in my refrigerator. Now, I trim off just the number of leaves I need for a salad or a sandwich and leave the rest to keep growing. Couldn't be easier.

There are four main types of lettuces. Crisphead lettuces are tight, round heads, such as 'Great Lakes', 'Summertime', and 'Nevada'. Butterheads are looser heads such as 'Bibb', 'Buttercrunch', 'Tom Thumb', and 'Mignonette'. Loose-leaf lettuces are very loose leaves in a rosette, such as 'Black Seeded Simpson', 'Green Ice', 'Oak Leaf', 'Salad Bowl', 'Prizehead', and 'Ruby'. The last group is romaine, which grows in erect, cylindrical bunches and includes 'Medallion', 'Olga', and 'Parris Island' varieties. While all lettuces prefer cooler weather, loose-leaf and romaine varieties are more heat-tolerant than the others.

Aside from their appeal on the table, lettuces can be a beautiful addition to the garden. A row of head lettuces makes a striking border for a flower

bed. Mesclun can be a colorful container crop. Small head lettuces such as 'Tom Thumb' can fill in small gaps in an edible or ornamental garden and benefit from the shading of taller plants nearby. If you think of lettuce not just as an edible, but also as an attractive foliage plant, all kinds of planting opportunities will present themselves.

When to Plant

In cold-winter areas, sow lettuce seeds after the last frost as soon as the soil is workable. In areas with mild winters and cool summers, sow seeds in early spring to harvest in spring and summer or in late summer for harvest in fall and winter. In areas with mild winters but hot summers, lettuce is best grown as a winter/early spring crop. In California, it's possible to have a lettuce harvest through the winter using a cold frame or hoop house (which is a protected plant bed/greenhouse with a plastic roof wrapped over flexible piping).

Where to Plant

Lettuces can be grown throughout California. Plant in full sun or in partial shade in the hottest regions. The soil should be loose, well drained, and amended with organic matter.

How to Plant

Before planting, add compost or an all-purpose fertilizer and work it several inches into the soil. Broadcast the seed and barely cover it with a light sprinkling of soil. Tamp down to ensure seeds make contact with the soil and water until moist. Seeds germinate in five to fourteen days. Thin seedlings to 6 inches apart or more, depending on the variety.

Mesclun mixes, which are an assortment of young salad greens, should be broadcast in blocks and should not be thinned since they will be harvested while they're still young.

To prolong the harvest, repeat the sowings every two weeks throughout the cool spring and fall weather.

Care and Maintenance

Keep the lettuce bed lightly but consistently moist. Feed with a light fish emulsion at the time of planting and again six weeks later.

Lettuce beds can be very appealing to snails, slugs, and earwigs, which would just love to beat you to the harvest. Liberal sprinkling of diatomaceous earth can keep them in check. Whiteflies can also be a problem, but they are best handled with yellow sticky traps.

Harvesting

Depending on the variety, lettuces can be ready to harvest in thirty-five to sixty-five days from sowing. Harvest head lettuces as soon as the heads

reach a good size. If you leave them in the ground much beyond that point they will quickly bolt and become bitter-tasting. Loose-leaf and romaine lettuces can be harvested by clipping the outer leaves as needed so that new leaves can grow in the center, or by taking the entire bunch at once.

"Cut-and-come-again" lettuces are generally loose-leaf-type lettuces that are intended to be harvested well before maturity. When the leaves are a few inches high, cut across the leaves about ½ inch above the crowns of the plants. After harvesting, apply a light fish emulsion solution to encourage regrowth.

Additional Information

One of the biggest challenges to growing lettuce can be dealing with sudden heat waves that can quickly cause the lettuce to bolt. There are a few varieties, however, that are more heat-tolerant than others, such as 'Deer Tongue' and 'Marvel of Four Seasons', both butterheads; 'Reine de Glace', a crisphead; and 'Slowbolt', a loose-leaf lettuce.

If you want to add a little more zing to your salads, consider adding some other gourmet greens. Arugula (*Eruca sativa*, also called "rocket") is a peppery green that you can grow and harvest much the same way you do mesclun. If you leave a plant or two to grow to maturity and go to seed, it will reseed and you'll have a ready-made crop coming up the next growing season. A nutty-flavored alternative is mache (*Valerianella locusta*, also called "lamb's lettuce" or "corn salad"). This is another cool-weather crop that can be sown in midsummer in cold-winter regions or fall through winter in mild-winter regions. It's slower growing than lettuce, taking up to ninety days to mature, but it is more cold hardy, is resistant to mildew, and will reseed.

Endive (*Cichorium endivia*) is another gourmet green that can add some zing to a salad. Broadleaf endive (also called "escarole") is more heat-tolerant than lettuce and faster-growing in cold weather. Frisée (*Cichorium endivia* var. *crispum*) is a curly variety of endive that is slow to bolt and whose flavor mellows in cooler weather. In cold-winter areas, plant in late summer, and in mild-winter areas, plant in late summer/early fall.

Chickory and radicchio (*Cichorium intybus*), which is a red-leafed chickory, can add a slightly bitter tang to a salad. Green chickories can be sown in early spring. In mild-winter regions, you can plant additional crops in mid- to late summer. Most radicchio varieties can be also be sown in mid- to late summer.

LOQUAT

Odds are you've never seen a loquat (*Eriobotrya japonica*) in the supermarket, which is all the more reason why loquat trees are becoming ubiquitous in California. The evergreen trees are striking in the landscape, with rounded crowns and large, heavily veined leaves, and the small orange or yellow fruits favored in Asian cultures are increasingly popular here.

▓ When to Plant

Loquats are best planted in the rainy season but after danger of hard frosts has passed. The trees are hardy to 12°F but can handle frosts better after they've had a chance to get established.

▓ Where to Plant

Loquats can be grown in Zones 7–10 in California. Although trees will survive, they will not bear fruit in areas that are either too cool or too warm and moist. Loquats do best in full sun but can tolerate partial shade. They require good drainage but can tolerate a wide range of soil types. Loquat trees offer great landscaping possibilities as focal trees and can also do well in large containers or espaliered against a wall or fence.

▓ How to Plant

Loquat trees are shallow-rooted, and the roots should be handled with some care. Plant the tree in a hole as deep as the rootball and twice as wide. If it is at all rootbound, gently loosen or trim away circular roots. Fill the hole with loose soil and mulch heavily, keeping the mulch several inches away from the base of the trunk. Water deeply.

■ *Care and Maintenance*

The trees are drought-tolerant, but they will produce better fruit with regular deep watering, particularly when blossoms begin to swell and two or three times during the fruiting period. They also benefit from regular light applications of a balanced fertilizer, such as a 6-6-6 fertilizer, given three times a year. At a minimum, feed once a year in midwinter. Don't get carried away with feeding, however; too much nitrogen will reduce flowering and fruiting.

Grafted trees will begin to bear fruit in two to three years. After harvest, prune to control size and to let light into the center of the tree. Loquat trees can tolerate severe pruning, and although they can grow to 20 to 30 feet high, they are often kept closer to 10 feet for ease of harvesting.

Loquats don't usually have serious pest problems but can be damaged by fireblight, particularly in areas with late spring and summer rain or high humidity. Fireblight is a fungal disease that can be spread by bees and will cause scorched-looking branches. Prune off damaged wood (which should not be composted) and treat with a fungicide.

■ *Harvesting*

Loquat fruits grow in clusters, so for the best quality and bigger size, it's advisable to thin the fruit. Bagging the clusters of fruit on the tree can also help minimize damage from the sun and birds.

In California, loquats ripen between March and June, or ninety days following full flower opening. The fruit should ripen on the tree before being harvested. Ripe fruit will keep in the refrigerator for one to two weeks and can be eaten fresh or used to make jam, jelly, chutney, or wine. The fruit can be sweet, sweet-tart, or tart, depending on the variety. A five-year-old standard tree can yield as much as 100 pounds of fruit. Loquats often bear a light or no crop in alternate years.

■ *Additional Information*

Loquats are either orange-fleshed or white-fleshed. Recommended varieties for orange-fleshed fruit are 'Big Jim', 'Early Red', 'Gold Nugget', 'Mogi', 'Mrs. Cooksey', 'Strawberry', 'Tanaka', and 'Wolfe'. White-fleshed varieties are 'Advance', 'Benlehr', 'Champagne', 'Herd's Mammoth', 'Victory', and 'Vista White'.

'Gold Nugget' and 'Mogi' are self-fertile. 'Advance' and 'Champagne' are both self-infertile and can be cross-pollinated with 'Gold Nugget'. 'Champagne' is a good choice for hotter regions; 'Gold Nugget' is recommended for the cooler regions.

MELON

Melon is a general category that includes some of the most delicious fruits around: cantaloupes (also called "muskmelons") and honeydews (*Cucumis melo*), and watermelons (*Citrullus lanatus* var. *lanatus*). Probably originating in Africa, melons are heat-loving orbs that need two and a half to four months of high temperatures to develop that sweet, juicy, colorful flesh. They also need a bit of space, since the vines can grow up to 6 feet long. In the past I haven't had much success with melons in my temperate climate, but I've learned a few tips for maximizing the heat around melon vines that I plan on trying in the future. Maybe they'll work for you too.

When to Plant

Melons can be direct-seeded outdoors in the spring after all danger of frost has passed and nighttime temperatures are above 50°F.

Where to Plant

Cantaloupes and honeydews can be grown in Zones 4–11, watermelons in Zones 3–11. In addition to the heat requirement, melons prefer sandy, slightly acidic (pH 6.0–6.5) soil that's been amended with composted manure or an all-purpose fertilizer.

How to Plant

Direct-sow seeds 1 inch deep. Melons are often planted in hills with three seeds per hill that are then thinned to two seedlings per hill. If you plant in rows, seedlings should ultimately be 6 inches apart. Seeds can also be started indoors and transplanted, especially in areas with a short growing season.

Laying down black plastic sheeting as mulch helps warm the soil quite a bit, which can make a big difference in a milder climate. Floating row covers also add some warmth, but should be removed when the vines start to sprawl and flower.

Another way to increase the heat for melons is to plant them in raised beds or containers. Planting in a container sitting on a brick or concrete patio onto which the vines can spill onto helps warm them even more.

Because the vines can take up a lot of room, you may want to provide a structure for the vines to climb up. Unless you are growing a very small variety of melon, though, you will need to use some kind of sling to secure the melons to the structure as they grow.

Care and Maintenance

Keep the vines regularly watered, and if you use black plastic mulch, make sure the water is getting to the plant. Apply a fish emulsion solution or balanced fertilizer about six weeks after planting. Watch for beetles on the plants and for rodents chewing on the plants and fruit.

■ Harvesting

Watermelons begin ripening about three to four months after planting. When the spot on the bottom of the melon that rests on the ground turns yellow, check to make sure the melon feels heavy and that the rind is dull. That means it's time to pick.

With cantaloupes, the melon will smell sweet and the tendril and leaf near the stem will wither. Most will "slip" off the stem with little effort. With honeydews, the rind turns yellowish and gets dull, and the bottom will get slightly soft to the touch.

■ Additional Information

For cantaloupes, try 'Solid Gold', 'Ambrosia', 'Jenny Lind', and 'Minnesota Midget'. Recommended honeydew varieties include 'Super Dew' and 'Earlidew'. For watermelons, some home growers have more success growing "icebox" varieties—smaller, round 4- to 7-pound melons that can have yellow, orange, or red flesh. Try 'Petite Yellow', 'Sweet Siberian', 'New Orchid', 'Yellow Doll', or 'Tiger Baby'. For larger melons try 'Moon and Stars', 'Blacktail Mountain', or 'Orangeglo'.

OKRA

I confess that I had never seen an okra plant (*Abelmoschus esculentus*) until the year when I toured a school garden in Dallas. I was surprised to see that the plants are so large, growing up to 7 feet tall, and rather attractive with their hibiscus-like flowers—almost as surprised as I was to find that there are children who actually eat okra. It is the green (or sometimes white or red) seedpod that is the edible part of the plant, and it is particularly popular throughout the southern states, where it is often used in soups and gumbos. Maybe someday someone will turn me on to a fabulous recipe that will change my mind about this odd-looking vegetable with a reputation for sliminess. But until then, I'll happily let you have my share of all the world's okra.

■ When to Plant

Okra needs warm soil to germinate, so wait until all danger of frost has passed and the ground has warmed to 70°F to sow seeds.

■ Where to Plant

You can grow okra throughout California. Plant in full sun in well-drained soil. Amend the soil with compost before planting. The plants are bushy and tall, so be sure to allow enough room for the plant to grow where it won't shade out other plants.

■ How to Plant

To speed up germination, soak seeds for twenty-four hours before planting. Only plant the seeds that swell up after soaking. Sow the seeds ¾ inch deep and 6 inches apart in rows 2½ to 4 feet apart. When seedlings are a few inches high, thin to 1 to 1½ feet apart.

■ Care and Maintenance

Okra needs regular water, and mulch will help keep moisture in the ground and

suppress weeds. Feed the plants with an all-purpose fertilizer when the first pods set and again when the plants are 4 to 5 feet high.

Harvesting

Using a knife or a pair of pruners, begin harvesting the pods when they are 2 to 3 inches long, about fifty-five to sixty days from planting. You'll need to use gloves to handle the prickly skinned pods. Be sure to gather the pods when they are young because they get tough and woody as they age. Continue to harvest every couple days; if you stop picking, the plants will stop producing. Okra will keep in the refrigerator for several days and can also be frozen.

Additional Information

Recommended green okra varieties include 'Annie Oakley', 'Cajun Delight', 'Star of David', 'Cow Horn', 'Louisiana Short', 'Burmese Okra', 'Jade', and 'Emerald'. Red varieties are 'Red Burgundy', 'Alabama Red', and 'Hill Country Heirloom Red'. 'Silver Queen Okra' bears whitish green pods. 'Clemson Spineless' is a variety lacking the prickly characteristics that most other okras have.

OLIVE

Olive trees (*Olea europaea*) go back a long way in this state, at least to the days of the California Missions, where olive trees were included in the mission gardens. The California climate is so well suited to olive growing that the state is now seeking to become one of the world's leading producers of olive oil. For most home growers, however, making your own olive oil is not practical—you would need a huge amount of olives and a good deal of equipment to produce even a little bit of oil. But if you're willing to do the processing work that's required to make the fruit edible, homegrown, home-cured olives are certainly possible.

When to Plant

Plant new olive trees in the spring after the danger of frost has passed.

Where to Plant

Olive trees can grow in Zones 9–11. They require high heat and some winter chill but no late frosts that can kill blossoms. They are hardy to 15°F. Plant in full sun in deep, well-drained neutral soil. Olive trees can be grown in large containers or espaliered against a fence or wall. Do not plant the trees near patios or driveways where the fruit can leave dark stains.

How to Plant

Olive trees are shallow-rooted, and the roots should be handled with some care. Plant the tree in a hole as deep as the rootball and twice as wide. If it is

at all rootbound, gently loosen or trim away circular roots. Fill the hole with loose soil and mulch heavily, keeping the mulch several inches away from the base of the trunk. Water deeply and mulch.

Care and Maintenance

These drought-tolerant trees can get by with very little water, but in arid climates will benefit greatly from deep watering at least twice a year—once when flowering in the spring, and again in the fall before harvesting. Monthly watering is even better. Fertilizing is not essential, but application of a high-nitrogen fertilizer each spring is a good idea.

In the first year, you should prune to establish a single trunk or multiple trunks. After the first year, the tree should be pruned annually to keep the tree short enough to make harvesting easier. Olive trees will fruit in alternate years unless pruned moderately each year. Fruit usually grows on the previous year's growth and never grows in the same place twice, so pruning following a harvest will help you prune without inhibiting the next year's crop.

Olives are bothered by olive fruit flies, which can generally be controlled by cleaning up fruit from the ground and removing fruit left on the tree in winter. The trees are also susceptible to verticilium wilt and olive knot, a bacterial disease that can be spread by using infected pruning tools.

Harvesting

Olive trees usually begin bearing fruit in four years. To get bigger olives, thin the fruits when they are still quite small. The crop will ripen in late fall, but olives for curing should be picked while they're still green. (The black color of cured olives comes from being exposed to air after being cured with lye.) Handpick the olives to avoid bruising.

There are four methods for curing olives: lye curing, water curing, dry salt curing, and Greek-style curing. For more information on processing olives, check out this information from U.C. Davis: http://anrcatalog.ucdavis.edu/pdf/8267.pdf.

Additional Information

When selecting an olive tree, be sure you are purchasing a fruiting variety. Some varieties, such as 'Arbequina', and 'Mission', are self-fruitful, but even those will produce a better crop with another variety to cross-pollinate. Recommended varieties for olives for curing include 'Arbequina', 'Leccino', 'Manzanillo', 'Mission', 'Ascolano', 'Barouni', 'Gordal', 'Picholine', and 'Sevillano'.

ONION

I have heard rumors that there are actually people out there who do not care for onions. Different strokes for different folks, I guess, but I don't understand how they manage. Onions (*Allium cepa*) seem to be a key ingredient to an awful lot of savory cooking and rather hard to avoid. I would never try. While I can understand limiting one's intake of raw onions, dishes like French onion soup and pizza with caramelized onions and fried onion rings are mellow, rich, even sweet—and an excellent reason to grow a few in your garden.

Onions are categorized by the amount of hours of daylight they require to form a bulb. Long-day varieties require fourteen to sixteen hours of daylight and really are not suited for California growing. Intermediate-day varieties need twelve to fourteen hours and grow well in Central California. Short-day onions require only ten to twelve hours of sunlight; they are suitable for Southern California gardens. Bunching onions (also called scallions) never form an actual bulb. They can grow anywhere.

■ When to Plant

In mild-winter regions, sow seeds fall to early winter. Sets (small bulbs) and transplants can be planted throughout winter into early spring.

In cold-winter areas start seeds indoors in late winter. Plant sets and transplants in early spring.

Seeds will mature in one hundred ten to one hundred twenty-five days, transplants in seventy to ninety days, and sets in fifty to sixty days.

■ Where to Plant

Plant in loose, well-drained soil that is high in organic matter. Onions need at least six hours of sun a day.

■ How to Plant

Onions can be grown from seed, sets, or transplants. Growing from seed gives you a much larger crop for less money and you'll have a greater choice of varieties. Beginning gardeners may have greater success with sets and transplants. (More often than not, sets are only available in long-day varieties, but these can be grown in California to the green onion, or scallion, stage and harvested that way.)

Sow seeds ¼ inch deep in rows 15 to 18 inches apart. When seedlings are a few inches tall, thin to 4 to 5 inches apart.

Sets and transplants should be planted 4 to 5 inches apart or closer if you want to harvest some early as green onions. Bury sets just below the soil surface so that the point of the bulb is visible.

■ Care and Maintenance

Onions need consistent watering and benefit from mulching and diligent weeding. Uneven watering may cause the bulbs to split. Apply a balanced fertilizer or fish emulsion solution regularly, especially early in the growing season.

Pests include thrips, winged sucking insects that can be controlled with Neem, and onion root maggots, which bore into the onion bulb and can be controlled with diatomaceous earth.

■ Harvesting

Bulb onions are ready to harvest when the green tops turn yellow and fall over. Carefully dig up the bulbs using a garden fork and leave them to cure on top of the ground for about a week. Cover the bulbs with the tops to keep them from getting sun damaged. When the bulbs are completely dry, pull off the tops and wipe off the dirt. Store the bulbs in a cool, dark, well-ventilated place until you're ready to use them.

■ Additional Information

Short-day onions are usually sweeter than long-day types. Recommended varieties include 'Bermuda', 'California Red', 'Granex', 'Grano', 'Super Sweet', and 'Cipollini'.

Intermediate-day varieties include 'Autumn Spice', 'Red Torpedo', and 'Ringmaker'.

PARSLEY

Back in the days when the only parsley I knew was the curly kind that my mother insisted on putting atop her potato salad, I used to think of it as decorative but kind of useless. So not true. Parsley (*Petroselinum crispum*), which includes both the curly- and the flat-leaf, or Italian, varieties, is high in vitamins A and B, iron, and antioxidants. As a biennial plant, parsley will grow to 6 to 24 inches high the first year, then flower, set seed, and die in the second year. In some climates, however, it will act more like a herbaceous perennial, dying back to the ground in winter and then sending out new shoots in spring. Parsley is also used as a companion plant, particularly with tomatoes, for its ability to attract predatory insects that control pests such as tomato hornworms.

When to Plant

Sow seeds in spring for harvest through fall. In mild-winter climates, another crop can be planted in late summer.

Where to Plant

Parsley can be grown throughout California. Although it is more shade-tolerant than most herbs, it prefers full sun, or partial shade in hot-summer climates. It prefers rich, well-draining soil.

▪ How to Plant

Seeds can be started indoors, but because parsley has a taproot, which makes it more difficult to transplant, it's best to direct-seed it outdoors. It is very slow to germinate, sometimes taking from three to six weeks. Soaking the seeds for 24 hours before planting can speed up germination, but your crop is still likely to sprout over a period of weeks rather than all at once. When seedlings do appear, thin to 3 to 4 inches apart.

▪ Care and Maintenance

Keep the bed consistently moist and weeded. Fertilize regularly with a high-nitrogen fertilizer. Parsley can tolerate light frosts and can even overwinter in Zones 9–10.

Parsley attracts some types of swallowtail butterflies, which lay eggs on the leaves. The black-and-green striped caterpillars with yellow dots that result munch away on the leaves. You can use floating row covers to control the damage, but I'd suggest just planting enough extra parsley for both you and the caterpillars.

▪ Harvesting

Once the plant has developed four to five healthy stems, you can begin harvesting leaves and continue to harvest throughout the year. When the plant begins to flower the second year, pinch out the blossoms to keep it from setting seed and prolong the harvest. Parsley can be chopped and frozen in ice cube trays and stored in zip-lock bags in the freezer.

▪ Additional Information

Favored varieties of Italian flat-leaf parsley include 'Giant Italian', 'Single', 'Survivor', and 'Titan'. For curly parsley, which makes an attractive flower border, try 'Favorit', 'Forest Green', and 'Moss Curled'.

Hamburg parsley is a type used for its strong-tasting leaves, but primarily for its thick root, which has a nutty, celery-like flavor and is harvested in the fall. In central and Eastern European countries, it is cooked into soups and stews, but it can also be eaten raw, chopped into salads and slaws.

PARSNIP

Parsnips (*Pastinaca sativa*) are carrots' paler, even sweeter relatives. Originating in Siberia and Europe, parsnips are a cold-hardy vegetable with white to yellow roots that have a creamy, buttery flavor that has been described as similar to butterscotch. How many vegetables can you say that about? Frost only improves the flavor, and in colder regions, parsnips can be overwintered and enjoyed straight from the ground. High in potassium and dietary fiber, parsnips can be used to thicken soups and stews or roasted like other root vegetables.

When to Plant

In cold-winter areas, sow seeds in late spring for a fall harvest. You can leave parsnips in the ground through the winter and harvest as needed because the cold enhances the parsnips' sweetness.

In mild-winter regions sow parsnip seeds in fall to harvest in spring. Roots will get tough if left in the ground beyond the spring.

Where to Plant

Parsnips can be grown in all zones in California if planted at the right time. Plant in full sun in sandy loam that has been well worked over to make sure it is loose and stone-free to a depth of 15 inches. In areas with heavy clay soil, plant in raised beds or deep containers.

How to Plant

Parsnip seeds have a short shelf life and a poor germination rate, so be sure to use seed packaged for the current year and discard any seed not used at the end of the season. Soak seeds for 24 hours before planting. Sow seeds ¼ to ½ inch deep in rows 2 feet apart. Spread seed thickly (as much as two to three seeds per inch) to make up for the poor germination rate. It may take as long as twenty days for germination to occur.

Care and Maintenance

Keep parsnips evenly watered but not soggy, about 1 inch of water per week. Overwatering can cause the roots to grow hairy or forked. When seedlings are a few inches high, thin to 3 inches apart. After thinning, run a thin row of a balanced fertilizer down the row, about 2 inches from the seedlings. Keep the area weeded and watch for swallowtail butterfly caterpillars, which feed on the greens. These can be handpicked to control.

▓ *Harvesting*

Using a garden fork or shovel, harvest the roots when they reach 1½ to 2 inches in diameter and approximately 8 to 10 inches in length, usually around one hundred five to one hundred fifty days. A frost will encourage root starch to convert to sugar, which enhances the flavor. A typical yield is about a pound of parsnips per foot row.

▓ *Additional Information*

Recommended varieties include 'All American', 'Cobham Improved Marrow', 'Harris Model', 'Hollow Crown', 'Andover', 'Lancer', 'Avonreister', 'Countess', 'Gladiator', 'Javelin', and 'Tender and True'.

Parsnips contain compounds that can cause a skin irritation in some people called parsnip rash, or phytophotodermatitis. The rash can make the skin sensitive to light and lead to severe burning. To avoid any problem, only handle parsnip plants when wearing long sleeves and gloves. (The roots themselves can usually be handled without any problem.) If your skin does come in contact with the plant and a rash occurs, wash the irritated area; cover it with a cool, wet cloth; and do not expose the affected area to sunlight until the rash has cleared.

PASSION FRUIT

While the passion flower vine is grown just for its remarkable blossoms, the related passion fruit vine (*Passiflora edulis*) offers both remarkable flowers and exotic fruit. The evergreen vine can climb 20 to 30 feet high, covering a wall or tall fence with lush greenery and white blossoms with white and purple crowns, followed by round, fragrant fruits. Those fruits are rich in vitamins C and A, iron, and potassium and are said to have somniferous properties—drink a little passion fruit juice before bed and you may have a more restful and relaxing night's sleep.

■ When to Plant

In regions that have frosts, plant in the spring after all danger of frost has passed. In frost-free areas, passion fruit vines can be planted at any time.

■ Where to Plant

Passion fruits can be grown in Zones 8–10 in California. They need well-drained soil that is rich in organic matter and low in salt. Ideal soil pH is 6.5 to 7.5, but it can adapt to a wide range of soil types. The vine must be planted where it will have a trellis or other support to grow on and protection from the wind.

How to Plant

Most of the commercially sold passion fruit vines are hybrids grafted onto rootstock for greater resistance to root disease. Grafted plants are also much hardier and longer-lived. Plant the grafted vine in a hole as deep and twice as wide as the rootball, taking care not to cover the graft union. Mulch and water well.

Although it is not the preferred method, you can also grow the plants from seed. If you use seed taken directly from the fruit, it will usually germinate in two to three weeks. Older seeds will germinate more slowly, although you can speed germination by nicking the seed with a nail file or rubbing it with sandpaper before planting.

Care and Maintenance

Passion fruit vines should be watered regularly until the winter, then not watered during the cold months. Pruning should be done each year after harvest. Cut excess stems back all the way to the ground and reduce the other stems by a third. The vines should be fed four times a year with a high-potassium fertilizer, such as a 10-5-20 NPK fertilizer.

Pests are less of a problem with passion fruit vines in California than in other places, but snails can be a significant problem. Nematodes can also be a severe threat and can shorten the life of the vine. The plants are also susceptible to fusarium if they're planted in infected soil.

Harvesting

The fruits of the passion fruit vine ripen in summer and fall when the rinds turn quickly from green to deep purple or red. The fruit will soon fall from the vine once it's ripe, so it must be harvested quickly. The pulp of the ripe fruit is orange, and it has a citrusy flavor. The pulp and the seeds are edible and can be eaten directly from the rind with a spoon, although it is most often used for juice.

There is also a yellow passion fruit, which is slightly larger, but the fruit is considered less desirable than the purple/red fruit.

Additional Information

Passion fruit vines are self-fruitful and do not need a cross-pollinizer. The recommended varieties include 'Red Rover' and 'Frederick' for the red-skinned fruit and 'Edgehill', 'Kahuna', 'Black Knight', 'Paul Ecke', and 'Purple Giant' for purple-skinned fruit. 'Edgehill' is particularly recommended for Southern California. 'Black Knight' is a good choice for container growing.

PEAS

Peas (*Pisum sativum*) are often a gardener's favorite edible, and I hear people report that the biggest problem they have is restraining themselves and others from eating the entire crop right off the vine before they ever make it to the kitchen. There are three broad categories of peas: shelling peas, which are harvested for the seeds inside the pods; edible-podded peas, which are harvested before the seeds have matured; and peas that are a combination of the two. Peas can be grown in bush form or on vines that climb up to 6 feet by curling tendrils (which are also edible).

▨ *When to Plant*

In cold-winter areas, sow seeds in early spring as soon as the ground can be worked. For a fall crop, sow seeds twelve weeks before the average first frost date.

In mild-winter areas, peas can be planted anytime from fall to early spring. To extend the harvest, do successive plantings several days apart.

▨ *Where to Plant*

Peas can be grown throughout California, but they do best in areas with long, cool springs. They can tolerate light frosts, but hot weather can lead to mildew problems and low yields.

Plant in full sun, or in afternoon shade in the hottest regions. Peas prefer well-draining soil that's been amended with compost and bonemeal or rock phosphate.

▨ *How to Plant*

Soaking seeds overnight prior to planting speeds up germination. In winter, sow seeds ½ to 1 inch deep. At other planting times, sow seeds 2 inches deep in light (sandy) soil, ½ to 1 inch deep in heavy (clay) soil. For bush peas, space the rows 2 feet apart. For vines, allow 5 feet between rows. Water the ground before planting, then withhold supplemental water until seedlings begin to emerge, which should occur in as few as six or as many as thirty-six days.

▨ *Care and Maintenance*

As the seedlings grow, keep the soil evenly moist but not soggy. Overhead watering can often lead to mildew problems, so drip irrigation or soaker hoses are recommended. Because peas create their own nitrogen, additional fertilizer is usually not necessary. If the soil is particularly sandy, one application of a balanced fertilizer six weeks after planting can be beneficial.

Peas are vulnerable to pea weevils, aphids, and thrips. Neem oil can usually keep infestations under control. Disease problems include powdery

mildew (particularly in hot weather), fusarium wilt, and pea enation mosaic virus. Planting disease-resistant varieties is really the only way to combat the last two.

Harvesting

Peas will generally be ready for harvest sixty to seventy days after planting, or three weeks after the blossoms appear. Pick all the pods that are ready, because if the pods are left on the vine to ripen, the plant will stop producing. For shelling peas, harvest when the pods swell up but before their bright green color begins to fade. For edible-podded peas, harvest when the pods are 2 to 3 inches long but before the seeds swell. Harvest time lasts two to six weeks from one planting, and vining peas can be expected to have the longest harvesting period. A typical yield would be 2 to 3 pounds of peas from a 15-foot row over a one-week period.

Additional Information

For shelling peas, recommended varieties include 'Mr. Big', 'Green Arrow', 'Maestro', 'Alderman', 'Garden Sweet', 'Survivor', 'Thomas Laxton', and 'Wando'. Also favored are the smaller, French variety of shelling peas known as *petits pois*. The varieties include 'Waverex' and 'Precovelle'.

For edible-podded peas (sugar or snow peas), try 'Mammoth Melting Sugar', 'Oregon Giant', 'Oregon Sugar Pod II', and 'Snow Wind'.

There also varieties that are a combination of shelling and edible-podded peas. These include 'Super Sugar Snap', 'Sugar Ann', and 'Sugar Lace'.

PEACH

Do you dare to grow a peach (*Prunus persica*)? Who wouldn't want to have a crop of these sweet, juicy fruits each year, yours just for the picking? Oh, if only it were that simple. Growing peaches presents a few challenges. They are attractive to a number of pests and prone to many diseases. They require heavy pruning, and harvesting can be demanding work because there's a short window of time to get all the fruit in. And forget about growing them anywhere with very cold winters. But if you can get past all that, read on—there may be a peach that will suit you just fine.

The same growing conditions (and warnings) that apply to peaches also apply to nectarines (*Prunus persica* var. *nucipersica*).

■ When to Plant

Bare-root trees are available in nurseries in late winter, and you can usually find trees in containers through the summer. The best time to plant is before the tree begins to leaf out. (Watch for slight swelling at the leaf nodes along the branches to signal that dormancy is breaking.)

■ Where to Plant

Peaches and nectarines will grow in Zones 5–9, depending on the amount of chill needed. Most varieties require 600–900 chill hours; in milder climates look for low-chill varieties. Plant in full sun in very well-drained soil that is rich in organic matter.

■ How to Plant

Plant in a hole twice as wide and the same depth as the rootball. Take care that the graft union at the bottom of the trunk is above the soil line. When planting a very young, branchless tree, prune it back to 2 to 3½ feet high to encourage a good branching system. Water well and mulch.

■ Care and Maintenance

Trees should be pruned to an open vase shape while they're still young. Pruning in early spring just as dormancy is breaking is best so that the cuts heal quickly and are less susceptible to disease. Peaches and nectarines bear fruit on one-year-old wood, so yearly pruning is necessary to keep the tree fruiting. Remove about one-third of the new growth each year. Make sure that the tree has good circulation through the center to minimize the risk of disease.

Peach leaf curl, brown rot, and powdery mildew are the most serious diseases affecting peaches and nectarines. These fungal diseases can usually be controlled by keeping the ground and tree clean and by applying copper or lime sulfur sprays while the tree is dormant. Combining horticultural oil with the lime sulfur can help control certain pests such as scale and plum curculio. The most serious pests are peach tree borers, which can bore holes into the trunk and kill it. Periodically inspect the base of the trunk for holes, and if you find them, contact your Cooperative Extension office for information on treating them.

Harvesting

When peaches and nectarines are fully colored with no green left on the skin, they're ready to harvest. You should be able to pluck it easily from the tree, and it should give slightly when pressed. The fruit doesn't keep for long on the tree and it bruises easily, so you have to harvest it quickly and carefully. A mature, standard-size tree can yield 100 to 150 pounds of fruit each year.

Additional Information

Both peaches and nectarines have large pits that are either loose (freestone) or attached to the flesh (cling). The varieties recommended here are freestone and self-fruitful unless otherwise indicated.

For peaches, try 'Frost' (moderate chill), 'Arctic Supreme' (high chill), 'Madison' (high chill), 'Suncrest' (moderate chill), or 'Tropic Snow' (low chill).

Recommended nectarine varieties include 'Arctic Star' (semi-freestone, low chill), 'Cavalier' (moderate chill), 'Southern Belle' (dwarf, low chill), 'Goldmine' (low chill), and 'Zee Glo' (moderate chill).

PEAR

For a long time it seemed Americans were doomed to have only one pear in their lives—'Bartlett'. In recent years a few more varieties have been showing up in supermarkets, usually 'Bosc' or 'Comice'. But with antique varieties dating back to the 1700s, most of us still have a lot to learn (and taste) when it comes to pears. European pears (*Pyrus communis*) are rather sensitive fruits, which is why you don't see very many varieties in the supermarkets—they don't ship well. Asian pears (*Pyrus pyrifolia*), on the other hand, are firmer and crisper with a texture that is more like a very juicy apple.

Growing to their full size of 30 to 40 feet, pear trees make great shade trees, but with regular, proper pruning they can be kept as small as 6 feet for easy harvest. They can also be espaliered or trained as a hedge.

When to Plant

Bare-root trees are available in nurseries in late winter and you can usually find trees in containers through the summer. The best time to plant is while the tree is still dormant.

Where to Plant

Pears can grow in Zones 4–9. Plant in full sun. Most pears prefer well-draining soil, but can tolerate heavier soil. (If the pear is grafted onto quince rootstock, however, it will not bear well in poorly draining soil.)

How to Plant

Plant in a hole twice as wide and the same depth as the rootball. Take care that the graft union at the bottom of the trunk is above the soil line. Water well and mulch. Prune off the top third of the tree to encourage better root formation and a healthier tree structure.

Care and Maintenance

Unless in a region that receives a good deal of summer rain, pear trees need deep watering about once a month. Reapplying mulch each year will help keep the moisture in the soil. Avoid high-nitrogen fertilizers, which will encourage growth that is susceptible to fireblight and freezes.

Shape young trees to a modified central leader with three or four main lateral branches. Prune annually to maintain the shape, remove dead wood and water sprouts (vertical branches that don't bear fruit), and keep the tree open to sunlight and good air circulation. Fruit grows on wood spurs that produce for many years, but once the trees are established, you should remove about 10 percent of the spurs each year.

Fireblight is one of the more severe threats for pears. Remove the affected branches, which look scorched, destroying the clipped wood and disinfecting your pruning tools afterward. Other problems include codling moths, pear psylla, scale, and scab.

■ Harvesting

Most pears ripen in summer and fall, although they can take four to six years to produce their first crop. Pears should be thinned when still small to prevent disease and grow bigger fruit. Pick European pears when they are still firm and just starting to change color. Asian pears should be picked fully ripe; they will not ripen further after picking. Full-sized pear trees can yield 150 to 250 pounds of fruit a year.

Some European pears are harvested in the winter, like 'Comice', and need to be cured for three to four weeks at 32°F without freezing. Winter pears can be stored for as long as four months.

■ Additional Information

Many pears need a pollinizer as well as a fair amount of winter chill. Recommended European pear varieties include 'Bartlett' (800 chill hours, self-fruitful), 'Bosc' (700 chill hours, needs a pollinizer), 'Comice' (600 chill hours, self-fruitful), 'Seckel' (700 chill hours, self-fruitful), and 'Warren' (500 chill hours, needs a pollinizer). For Asian pears, try 'Kosui' (900 to 1,000 chill hours, needs a pollinizer), 'Shinseki' (450 chill hours, self-fruitful), and 'Tsu Li' and 'Ya Li' (300 chill hours, pollinize each other).

PECAN

Pound for pound, planting a pecan tree (*Carya illinoensis*) might be one of the most cost-efficient things you could do in your garden. Growing to 75 to 100 feet tall, these large, stately trees are not only beautiful in the landscape, but they produce prodigious amounts of expensive nuts that are high in protein, omega-6 fatty acids, and antioxidants. Best of all, they make one heck of a pie.

When to Plant

Plant pecan trees in the winter when the trees are dormant.

Where to Plant

Pecans can be grown in Zones 5–9 in California. They do best in inland areas with long, hot summers. Plant in full sun in well-drained soil; they can't tolerate salt in the soil. Pecans have very deep roots, so they should be planted only where the root systems will be able to grow to a depth of 6 to 10 feet. Plant the trees at least 40 feet apart and 20 feet away from other structures (foundations, sidewalks, driveways, or power lines).

How to Plant

Pecan trees have long taproots and must be handled carefully when planting. Make sure the hole is as deep as the rootball and twice as wide and the graft union is above the soil level. Fill in the soil around the rootball, making sure the tree is straight, and water well.

■ Care and Maintenance

Pecan trees need an ample supply of soil water for good growth and nut production. In the first year, apply a high-nitrogen fertilizer in June. Over the next three years apply the fertilizer again in April, May, and June. Never fertilize a pecan after June. Pecans also benefit from a 2- or 3-inch layer of mulch each spring.

If you spot signs of chlorosis in the leaves (yellow between the veins), apply a foliar spray with zinc two or three times in the spring.

Pecans should be pruned to a strong central leader. Prune to establish the structure in the first few years; after that, only light pruning is needed to remove dead wood and suckers and keep the shape.

■ Harvesting

Pecan trees do not produce nuts for the first five to seven years, and they produce a light or no crop in alternate years. Trees bloom in the late spring or early summer, and the nuts ripen in the fall. Harvesting is easy, but a little competitive. Just gather them from the ground after they drop. You may be in a race with the local wildlife to see who gathers the most nuts, but as the tree matures, there will likely be enough nuts to satisfy everyone. A ten-year-old tree produces about 10 pounds of nuts, but a fully mature tree can yield 100 pounds.

Before storing the nuts, spread them out in a thin layer on screens in an area that is warm but out of direct sunlight. Let them dry like that for two weeks, then store in airtight containers or freeze.

■ Additional Information

Pecans are divided into Type 1 and Type 2 varieties, and you generally need one tree of each type for cross-pollination. Type 1 varieties that do well in California include 'Cheyenne' and 'Pawnee'. Recommended Type 2 varieties include 'Western-Schley', 'Burkett', 'Mohawk', 'Wichita', 'Shoshani', and 'Kanza'.

PEPPER

How do you like it—sweet or hot? I'm talking about peppers, of course. It's amazing to think that one type of plant can produce fruit with such a range of flavor and spice. Like yin and yang, I think both types of peppers (*Capsicum* spp.) have their place—in the garden and in the kitchen. Whether you enjoy them as cool, crunchy salad additions or hot, stuffed peppers, life will be more flavorful if you plant some peppers.

When to Plant

Start seeds indoors eight to ten weeks before the average last frost date. Seedlings can be transplanted outdoors when the springtime night temperatures are above 55°F.

Where to Plant

Peppers can be grown in all zones in California, but they do best where there is a long, warm growing season. In the hotter regions like Zones 10–11, they can be grown as perennials; elsewhere they are usually annuals. Plant in full sun; in really hot, dry climates, they need afternoon shade.

How to Plant

Sow seeds ¼ inch deep and 1 inch apart in a flat of potting mix. Keep warm (80° to 85°F) and moist until seedlings are a couple inches tall. Thin the seedlings or transplant to individual pots. When the nighttime temperatures are above 55°F, the seedlings can be transplanted outdoors. Amend the soil with compost before planting. Space the peppers 2 feet apart; water well and mulch. Plants that bear larger peppers should be staked or caged for support. Peppers also grow well in containers and raised beds, where the soil stays warmer.

Care and Maintenance

In mild climates, pepper plants can be helped along by using a clear plastic mulch and floating row covers to keep the plants as warm as possible. Keep them moist, watering deeply once a week. After the plants are established outside but before they have set blossoms, apply a balanced fertilizer and repeat it again in midseason.

It is important that you not grow peppers in the same place two years in a row. Crop rotation will help keep the soil healthier and disease-free. Pests to watch for include aphids, whiteflies, and cutworms. Pepper weevils can be a serious problem; if plants become infested, they should be destroyed after harvest.

■ Harvesting

Peppers are usually ready to harvest in sixty to ninety-five days, although some hot peppers can take much longer. Cut the peppers from the plant using pruners. Sweet peppers can be picked green or when they are fully colored. The flavor will develop more as the color changes. Hot peppers need to ripen fully on the plant, with the exception of poblanos and jalapeños, which can be picked green. (Note: Peppers must be completely ripe to be dried or they will rot.)

■ Additional Information

Recommended sweet pepper varieties include 'California Wonder' (seventy-five days), 'Blushing Beauty' (seventy-five days), 'Baby Belle' (eighty days), 'Cherry' (ninety days), 'Golden Bell' (eighty days), 'Gypsy' (seventy days), 'Pimento' (ninety days), and 'Valencia' (sixty-eight days).

For hot peppers, try 'Spanish Padron' (eighty to eighty-five days), 'Bolivian Rainbow' (eighty days), 'Fish Pepper' (seventy-five days), 'Habanero' (one hundred forty days), 'Hungarian Hot Wax Banana' (eighty days), 'Jalapeño' (ninety days), 'Tabasco' (one hundred twenty days), and 'Thai Hot' (ninety days).

PERSIMMON

Persimmons (*Diospyros kaki*) are one of the wonders of fall. When the weather starts to turn cool, persimmon trees go ablaze in shades of bright yellow-orange or red. The fruits hang like glowing orange orbs, even after the last of the leaves have fallen.

In the West particularly, when people think of persimmons they're usually thinking of Asian persimmons. There are also native American persimmons, however, which are hardier but have much smaller fruit. While some persimmons are considered to be self-fertile, having another tree to act as a pollinizer generally improves the size of the harvest and the quality of the fruit.

When to Plant

Plant bare-root persimmon trees in the early spring. Container plants can be found later in the year and planted in the summer.

Where to Plant

Asian persimmons will grow in Zones 6–10. American persimmons are hardier and can grow in Zones 4–10. If you live in a colder region and want to grow an Asian persimmon, look for an Asian variety grafted onto American persimmon rootstock. Plant in full sun. (American persimmons will tolerate some shade.) It needs good drainage but can accommodate a range of soil types.

How to Plant

Plant in a hole twice as wide but no deeper than the rootball. Make sure soil does not come up higher on the trunk than it was in the container. Take care that roots do not dry out before planting and water well once planted.

Care and Maintenance

Water your persimmon tree regularly and fertilize with an all-purpose fertilizer in late winter or early spring. Too little or too much water, or too much fertilizing, can lead to fruit drop. Prune in the first three years to establish the shape of the tree, then in later years to remove dead wood and keep the shape.

▥ *Harvesting*

Persimmon trees can take up to six years to bear their first fruit. Regardless of the type of persimmon, it is best to harvest the fruit when they are still firm but fully colored and let them ripen fully indoors. Use clippers to remove the persimmons, taking care not to bruise them.

Persimmons are considered either astringent or non-astringent. American persimmons and some Asian varieties are astringent and need to ripen to the point that they have a soft, pudding-like consistency inside. At that point, you can slice off the top and eat the pulp inside with a spoon. Other Asian varieties like 'Fuyu' are non-astringent and will soften slightly but not as much as the astringent types. Persimmons can be eaten raw or cooked and can be frozen or dried.

▥ *Additional Information*

Be sure when choosing your persimmon that you consider whether it is American or Asian, and whether or not it needs a pollinizer. American persimmons and Asian persimmons cannot pollinize each other. American persimmons produce either male or female flowers, and you need both a male and a female tree to produce fruit. Asian varieties are more complicated, so check into what your selected variety needs in order to bear fruit.

The most popular Asian varieties are 'Fuyu', which is non-astringent and seedless, and 'Hachiya', which is astringent and usually seedless; neither of these need a pollinizer. Other options are 'Jiro', which is similar to 'Fuyu',

non-astringent and self-fertile; 'Saijo', which is astringent and self-fertile; and 'Sheng', non-stringent and self-fertile. 'Chocolate' is non-astringent but needs 'Nishimura Wave' as a pollinizer.

The following recommended American varieties are self-fertile, but having more than one will improve your harvest: 'Meader', 'Szukis', and 'Ruby'. 'Early Golden' is often, but not always, self-fertile.

'Russian Beauty' and 'Nikita's Gift' are Asian hybrids that are as hardy as American persimmons but with bigger fruit and excellent flavor.

PINEAPPLE GUAVA

Pineapple guava (*Feijoa sellowiana*) is about as accommodating as a plant can be, both in the garden and in the kitchen. An evergreen shrub that can be trained as a tree, it has gray-green leaves, pink-red blossoms, and green, egg-shaped fruits that drop at your feet when they're ready to be eaten. It can be left in all its shrubby fullness, pruned to a hedge, espaliered against a fence, or grown in a container. You can nibble its blossoms in the spring and its fruit in the fall, and it will adapt to just about any soil type or level of maintenance you care to provide.

When to Plant

Plant young trees in spring after danger of frost has passed. In areas without frosts, pineapple guavas can be planted at any time. They can also be grown from seed, but seedlings are slow growing and may not produce high-quality fruit.

Where to Plant

Pineapple guavas grow in Zones 8–11, but crops will be disappointing if they do not get at least 50 hours of winter chill. Plant trees in full sun, or in partial shade in the hottest regions. In colder regions, they can be grown in containers and brought indoors in the winter.

How to Plant

Plant in a hole twice as wide but no deeper than the rootball. Make sure that soil does not come up higher on the trunk than it was in the container. Take care that roots do not dry out before planting, and water well once planted.

Care and Maintenance

Pineapple guavas are very drought-tolerant, but the quality of the fruit diminishes without supplemental water. Feed lightly with an all-purpose fertilizer in the spring, and keep a layer of mulch around the tree. Severe pruning isn't necessary, but keep suckers trimmed from the base of the tree. A light pruning after the fruit is harvested will encourage new growth the following year. It grows slowly, and most varieties will reach 15 feet high and wide if left unpruned. Pineapple guavas have very little problem with pests other than scale, which can be managed by blasting with a spray of water or an application of Neem.

Harvesting

The fruit ripens in the fall and will drop off the tree when it is fully ripe and at its peak flavor. Fruit that is left on the ground will quickly become overripe. An easy way to collect the fruit is to spread a tarp below the tree when the fruit has begun to drop and then shake the branches so the ripe fruit falls onto the tarp. To eat the fruit, cut it in half and scoop the flesh out of the peel.

Pineapple guava flowers, which appear in the spring, are also edible, sweet-tasting, and fragrant. They can be used in salads or to make jams and jellies.

Additional Information

'Nikita' (a dwarf), 'Coolidge', 'Pineapple Gem', 'Beechwood', 'Mammoth', 'Nazemetz', and 'Trask' are all self-fruitful, but planting a cross-pollinizer will result in a heavier crop.

PLUM

Plums (*Prunus domestica*) are one of the most versatile fruits you can grow. They're good for baking, jams, chutneys, drying, and of course, eating fresh. Most plums fall into one of two categories—European or Japanese. Most plums are delicious eaten fresh, but the European plums have some of the best varieties for drying into prunes. Standard trees reach about 15 feet, but dwarf varieties top out at between 8 and 10 feet. They are lovely landscape trees when well pruned and shaped, and in the spring they put on a gorgeous show of white or pink blossoms.

When to Plant

Bare-root trees should be planted in winter while the tree is dormant. Container-grown trees are best planted in the fall.

Where to Plant

European plums can be grown in Zones 4–9, Japanese and hybrid plums in Zones 6–9. There are other plums that don't fall into either of these categories that tend to be hardier; they can be grown in Zones 3–9. Japanese plums generally require 500 to 900 hours of winter chill. European varieties need more—usually 700 to 1,000 hours.

Plant in full sun in rich, well-draining soil with a pH ranging from 6.0 to 8.0. European plums do better in heavier soils; Japanese plums prefer lighter soil.

How to Plant

Plant in a hole twice as wide and the same depth as the rootball. Take care that the graft union at the bottom of the trunk is above the soil line. Water well and mulch. Prune off the top third of the tree to encourage better root formation and a healthier tree structure.

■ Care and Maintenance

Deeply water plums every couple weeks (more in very hot weather). Try not to let the tree dry out for an extended period, but if it does and fruit has set, don't water until after harvest because the fruit will split. Apply a fresh layer of mulch each year. If the tree lacks vigor, you can apply a nitrogen fertilizer.

Prune plums to have an open center to allow light and air circulation. Japanese varieties require heavy pruning each year, while European and hybrid varieties can do with less.

In California, plums tend to have fewer pest and disease problems than do many other fruit trees, but you should still watch out for aphids and scale as well as fungal diseases. Peach tree borers can also attack plum trees; look for signs of small, dusty holes bored into the base of the trunk.

■ Harvesting

Japanese plums should be thinned to 4 to 6 inches apart to grow larger fruits. European varieties don't usually require thinning.

Plums ripen from May to September, depending on the variety. Pick European plums when they are completely ripe, fully colored, and a little bit soft to the touch. Japanese plums should be picked when fully colored but still slightly firm; they will finish ripening indoors.

■ Additional Information

Some plums are self-fruitful and some need a pollinizer, so do your research before you buy. Recommended European varieties include 'Damson' (400 chill hours, self-fertile), 'Green Gage' (500 chill hours, self-fertile), 'Italian Prune' (800 chill hours, self-fertile), and 'Stanley' (800 chill hours, self-fertile). For Japanese plums, try 'Burgundy' (250 to 400 chill hours, self-fertile), 'Au Roadside' (700 chill hours, self-fertile), 'Santa Rosa' (300 chill hours, self-fertile), and 'Weeping Santa Rosa' (400 chill hours, self-fertile).

There are also plum-apricot hybrids: pluots, plumcots, and apriums. Pluots are the most common of these. Look for 'Flavor Supreme' (500 to 600 chill hours, pollinize with any Japanese plum) and 'Dapple Dandy' (500 chill hours, pollinize with 'Flavor Supreme', 'Burgundy', or 'Santa Rosa').

POMEGRANATE

I loved pomegranates even before I knew they were good for me, and I've had the red-stained fingers to prove it. Pomegranates (*Punica granatum*) have recently become very popular as an antioxidant-rich superfood that's also high in vitamin C, potassium, and dietary fiber. But those juicy little red seed sacs that you have to pick out of their white rind have always been popular with me, and more so now that I know how fabulous they are sprinkled on spinach salads, stirred into oatmeal or yogurt, or blended into a smoothie. Pomegranate plants are also fabulous in the garden, with spectacular orange-red blossoms and bright green leaves that turn yellow in the fall. They are suitable for a low-water landscape plan and, once established, are relatively low maintenance as well.

When to Plant

The best times to plant a pomegranate are times when it is least likely to be stressed by weather extremes, namely spring and fall.

Where to Plant

Suitable for Zones 7–10, pomegranates do best in climates with cool winters and hot, dry summers. Plant in full sun; in partial shade they may grow and flower but not set fruit. They prefer well-drained, slightly acidic soil (pH 5.5 to 7.0), but can do well even in alkaline soil. They can be grown in containers, particularly in areas where frost protection is needed.

How to Plant

Plant in a hole twice as wide but no deeper than the rootball. Make sure soil does not come up higher on the trunk than it was in the container. Take care that roots do not dry out before planting, and water well once it's planted.

Care and Maintenance

Although they are drought-tolerant, the quality of the pomegranate fruits depends on getting adequate water at the right times. Newly planted trees should be watered every two to four weeks during dry spells, and mature trees benefit from occasional deep watering during dry periods as well. But do not water during dry spells when fruit is already set on the tree; this will cause the fruit to split.

The first year you should define the structure of the plant as a single- or multistemmed tree or shrub by selecting one, three, or five of the best stems emerging from the base and removing all the rest. Each year after that, prune out any new suckers, crossing branches, or dead wood in the spring.

Pomegranates seldom have serious pest problems, although the foliage may be attractive to deer.

Harvesting

Pomegranates ripen and become fully colored in late summer and into fall. Test one fruit for ripeness before picking more because they will not ripen further off the tree. Fully ripened fruit that is left on the tree will split. Pomegranates can be stored for several months in the refrigerator.

Additional Information

Hands down, the most commonly planted pomegranate in California is 'Wonderful', but other varieties to try are 'Utah Sweet', 'Granada', and 'Eversweet', which does better in cooler climates than 'Wonderful'. 'Nana' is a poplar dwarf variety (3 feet tall). There are other varieties to try as well, but be sure you are buying an edible fruit–bearing tree. Some varieties are ornamental only and don't bear any fruit at all or only bear fruit that is small and dry.

POTATO

To paraphrase Will Rogers, I never met a potato I didn't like. Having grown up on good old 'Russet', baked, roasted, or mashed, I've been delighted to discover that there is a whole rainbow of potatoes (*Solanum tuberosum*) out there: white, yellow, and blue flesh and brown, red, yellow, and purple skin. Even better, they're pretty easy to grow.

▦ When to Plant

In cold-winter areas, potatoes can be planted as soon as soil is workable in the spring. In mild-winter areas, plant in early spring for the summer crop, or in early fall to harvest in winter and spring. In areas that don't have severe frosts, crops can be planted in midwinter as long as there is still well-draining soil.

▦ Where to Plant

Potatoes can be grown throughout California. Plant in full sun in sandy, fast-draining, slightly acidic (pH 5 to 6) soil.

▦ How to Plant

The first step to a successful potato crop is buying certified disease-resistant seed potatoes. Cut them into 1½-inch cubes, each with at least two eyes. Small seed potatoes can be planted whole. Dry the potato pieces for a couple days, then plant them 2 inches deep and 1½ feet apart in loose, prepared soil. Water well. As the plants sprout and grow, add loose soil or compost around the stems, always being sure that the top leaves are still above the soil.

Another alternative planting method is to plant in 3- to 4-foot-high "towers" constructed of reed fencing, wrapped around large wire tomato cages. The seed potatoes are planted in a layer of compost mixed with straw, and then the tower is filled with more of the compost-straw mixture as the plants grow up. Because the plants grow so much taller this way, the yield can be two to three times larger than what you can get by growing potatoes in the ground. Potatoes also work well as a container crop, and some garden supply companies sell "grow bags" that make it easy to grow potatoes on a patio or deck.

Care and Maintenance

Keep the beds or towers evenly moist. Although you have to be on the watch for beetles and aphids, which can defoliate the plants, potatoes don't require much maintenance beyond watering and continuing to add compost mulch as the plants grow. Assuming you use certified disease-resistant seed potatoes, you shouldn't have to worry about blight, and crop rotation will help prevent most other diseases.

Harvesting

The growing time for potatoes runs anywhere from two to four months. You can begin to harvest early potatoes ("new" potatoes) when plants begin to bloom. If you want mature potatoes, wait until the plants die down. Use a garden fork to carefully dig the potatoes from the ground. If you planted in towers, you can just push the soil and mulch aside to see if they're ready for harvest and pull them out. In areas where the ground doesn't freeze, you can leave potatoes in the ground until you need them.

Additional Information

The variety to plant depends both on how you want to use the potatoes and where you are growing them. For baking and mashing, try 'Butte' and 'Russet Burbank'. 'Carola' is good for soup-making and 'Reddale' is good for boiling and stewing, or for salads. 'All Blue' is a beautiful bluish purple that looks great in salads.

For areas with short growing seasons, try 'Yukon' or 'Yukon Gold'. 'Nooksack' can handle particularly wet growing conditions better than most. If you have soil that seems prone to diseases, try 'Island Sunshine' (late blight resistant) or 'Reddale' (verticilium wilt resistant).

For container growing, recommended varieties include 'All Blue', 'Yukon Gold', 'Red Pontiac', or any fingerling varieties.

QUINCE

A relative of the pear, quince (*Cydonia oblonga*) has never gained the popularity of its cousins, largely because it is too hard and astringent-tasting to eat fresh. But once you cook it, something miraculous happens. It develops an apple-like flavor that is wonderful in sauces, pies, chutneys, jellies, and candies. You can use quince just the same way you would use apples; in fact, it is often cooked right along with apples or used as a substitute for apples.

Quince is pretty amazing in the landscape as well. It has soft pink blossoms in the spring and colorful fruits in the fall. Normally growing to 15 to 20 feet tall, it can also be espaliered or grown in a large container. Just be sure that you plant a fruit-bearing quince and not a flowering quince. While the flowering quince is beautiful in bloom, it's not as attractive overall as the common quince tree—and it doesn't deliver the goods.

When to Plant

Bare-root quinces can be planted in late winter and early spring. You can usually find trees in containers in the fall to plant then.

Where to Plant

Quince can be grown in Zones 3–9. They are hardy to –15°F. They are not a good option in warm, humid areas where they are highly susceptible to fireblight. Quince should be planted in full sun. They can tolerate less than good drainage, but in heavy clay or very sandy soils, they will not fruit well.

How to Plant

Plant in a hole twice as wide but no deeper than the rootball. Make sure soil does not come up higher on the trunk than it was in the container. Take care that roots do not dry out before planting, and water well once planted.

Care and Maintenance

Quince will tolerate droughts well enough, but for a better harvest, it's best to water regularly. Apply compost mulch each spring; that's really the only fertilizing it requires.

The quince tree is really more of a shrub, but you can shape it as a tree. Remove suckers from the crown and prune to keep the center of the tree open to sunlight. Pruning should be done in winter. Since the tree fruits on the tips of new growth, the tree can take heavy pruning if necessary. In areas where fireblight can be severe, however, you should prune lightly.

Watch for problems with the same pests that often bother apples— codling moth, curculios, scale, and borers. Fireblight is the most serious

disease that can afflict quince. Caused by bacteria, fireblight causes branches to look as though they've been scorched. If you see signs of fireblight, remove the affected branches, cutting away at least 8 inches below where the disease is present. Be sure to disinfect pruners or any other tools that come in contact with the diseased material, and burn or dispose of the diseased wood where it will not be composted.

Harvesting

The fruits ripen in the fall and are ready for picking when they turn color (yellow, orange, or green, depending on the variety) and become fragrant. Quince bruises easily, so handle with care when harvesting.

Additional Information

Quince trees are self-fertile. Some of the recommended varieties include 'Kaunching', 'Orange', 'Smyrna', 'Aromatnaya', 'Cooke's Jumbo', 'Havran', 'Pineapple', and 'Van Deman'.

RADISH

I have a hard time thinking of radishes without flashing on the scene from *Gone with the Wind* where a starving Scarlett O'Hara grabs one lone radish out of the ground, devours it hungrily, and then—well, never mind. While they may not be ideal on an empty stomach, radishes (*Raphanus sativus*) add a lot of *zing* to salads, stir-fries, and other dishes and are delicious all on their own as well. (Try roasting them—the flavor mellows and they become a whole new experience.) Radishes are ridiculously easy to grow, and home growers will find far more varieties available than they would ever find in the store. And like beets, radishes are a twofer vegetable: both the greens and the root are edible.

When to Plant

Radishes can be planted from seed in the spring as soon as the ground can be worked. In mild-winter regions, seed can also be sown in fall and winter. Successive crops can be planted weekly until the weather heats up. Heat will make the plants go to seed, and the roots become bitter-tasting.

Where to Plant

You can grow radishes anywhere in California. Plant in full sun or, in the hottest regions, in light shade. Radishes like rich soil with lots of organic matter, so prepare the bed by working in composted manure one month before planting.

■ *How to Plant*

Sow seeds ½ inch deep, 1 inch apart, in rows 1 to 1½ feet apart. Seeds can also be broadcast over the prepared bed. Seeds germinate in five to seven days. When seedlings reach 2 or 3 inches in height, thin every other plant. If you didn't add compost before planting, feed the seedlings ten days after planting with a fish emulsion solution.

■ *Care and Maintenance*

Consistent, even watering is important to achieve the best flavor. Keep the bed weeded. Floating row covers may be necessary to keep birds and flea beetles from getting to the seedlings.

■ *Harvesting*

For peak flavor, harvest and eat radishes as soon as the roots reach full size, which can be as early as three weeks or as long as two months. The longer they are left in the ground, the stronger the flavor will become.

■ *Additional Information*

There's so much more to radishes than the round, red balls we're used to seeing in grocery stores. Radishes can come in an assortment of shapes and colors, as well as sweeter flavors.

Round, white-fleshed varieties include 'Crimson Crunch' with bright red skin, 'Pink Punch' with magenta skin, and 'Easter Egg II' with a mix of white, pink, red, and purple skins.

So-called "breakfast radishes" are longer and cylindrical and sweeter in flavor. They include 'French Dressing', 'Red Flame', and 'Petit Dejeuner'.

Asian varieties called 'Beauty Heart' and 'Misato Rose Flesh' have watermelon-like colors—light green on the outside and red on the inside.

But if you really favor the more traditional red-on-the-outside, white-on-the-inside radish, look for 'Cherry Belle' and 'Cherriette'.

RHUBARB

You don't have to have a "vegetable garden" to grow rhubarb (*Rheum rhabarbarum*). With its large green leaves atop tall red or light green leafstalks, rhubarb is attractive enough to fit in in any ornamental garden. And as an easy-to-grow herbaceous perennial, it will last for years, providing crop after crop of sweet-tasting stems to cook for pies, jams, sauces, even wine. Cooked rhubarb can be frozen or canned, allowing you to enjoy your spring harvest well into winter. Just remember: rhubarb leaves contain oxalates, which are poisonous and can be lethal when consumed in large enough quantities. Be sure to cook and eat only the stems, not the leaves!

■ *When to Plant*

Plant rhubarb in late winter or early spring when bare-root rhizomes or container plants are available in nurseries. In the hottest regions, plant in fall for harvest in winter and spring.

■ *Where to Plant*

Rhubarb grows in Zones 2–8. Plant it in full sun, or in partial shade in the desert climates. It prefers slightly acidic (pH 6.0 to 6.8), well-draining soil that is rich in organic matter.

■ *How to Plant*

To plant divisions, dig holes 8 to 10 inches deep and about 3 to 4 feet apart. Mix the soil you've removed with an equal part of compost or composted manure. If your soil does not have good drainage, add in the same amount of sand. Refill the holes with soil mix, burying the roots with the tops set right at the soil line. Water well and mulch.

Rhubarb can be grown from seed, but it will not necessarily retain the same characteristics of the parent plant. To get the exact variety you want, you should plant root divisions.

■ *Care and Maintenance*

Rhubarb likes consistent water but does not like to be in soggy ground. Good drainage is essential, or the root crowns will rot.

Apply a balanced fertilizer in the spring and then mulch with compost or composed manure in the fall. Keep the area weeded so the plants don't have to compete for nutrients.

Rhubarb plants need to be divided every four to five years. Dig the plants up in the spring just when new growth has started to appear. Divide the crown into sections, making sure each section has at least one bud and 2 inches of root. Each crown can usually be divided into four to eight new divisions. Replant the divisions as directed above.

Harvesting

Allow the rhubarb plants to grow for two full seasons without harvesting stalks. In the third season, you can harvest stalks for four to five weeks in the spring. In subsequent springs, you can stretch the harvest time to eight weeks. Do not cut the stalks; instead, grasp them at the base, pulling sideways and outward. Never remove all the stalks from a plant. After harvesting, water and feed the plant with a balanced fertilizer. If any blossom stalks appear, cut them out.

Additional Information

'Victoria' is probably the most common variety of rhubarb grown. It is a heavy producer and has either red or green stalks. 'Crimson Red', 'Strawberry', 'Valentine', and 'McDonald' are also favorite varieties with bright red stalks.

SPINACH

It makes me a little sad to think of all the years I wasted not liking spinach (*Spinacea oleracea*). Like many kids, I'd taken one taste of that pile of wilted leaves, cooked to a grayish green and seasoned not at all, and said, "No way." Later on I discovered fresh spinach salads and realized that this highly nutritious vegetable had some culinary redeeming value after all. And then I learned to sauté/steam it in garlic-infused olive oil with sea salt and crushed red pepper and "No way" turned to "Where have you been all my life?" As a bonus, it's easy to grow—as long as you avoid growing it in the heat of summer, which will cause it to rapidly go to seed.

If you need further inducement to plant some spinach, keep in mind that commercially grown spinach is one of the Environmental Working Group's "Dirty Dozen"—the twelve fruits and vegetables most heavily contaminated with pesticides. That and the outbreaks of *E. coli* in packaged spinach make it worth planting a few rows of these great, good-for-you greens.

When to Plant

Sow seeds in fall or early spring. Spinach really does prefer the cool seasons. There are varieties that are adapted to tolerate heat better than others. Seeds can be started indoors or directly outside. Germination is best when soil temperatures reach 32° to 60°F and air temperatures are between 55° to 60°F. To prolong harvest, sow seeds in seven- to ten-day intervals.

Where to Plant

Spinach grows in all zones in California. Plant in full sun. In hottest areas, plant in partial shade.

How to Plant

Plant seeds ½ inch deep and 1 inch apart. Seeds should germinate in seven to ten days. Thin seedlings to 3 to 4 inches apart and then thin again to 6 inches apart. Consider the thinnings your first harvest!

Care and Maintenance

Spinach requires regular water, preferably through drip irrigation or soaker hoses to reduce risk of mildew. Keep the area free of weeds and mulched. Regular apply light feedings of a high-nitrogen fertilizer.

Leaf miners are the most common pests and are best prevented with yellow sticky traps that trap the adult flies. Spinach is also susceptible to fusarium wilt and powdery mildew. Fusarium wilt cannot be prevented if it is present in the soil, but some varieties are more resistant than others. Mildew is best controlled by preventing wet foliage conditions and planting resistant varieties.

Harvesting

Spinach reaches maturity at about forty days. To harvest, cut individual outer leaves, leaving the inner leaves to keep growing, or cut the entire bunch at ground level.

Additional Information

There are three types of spinach: Savoy, with dark, crinkled, and curly leaves; flat or smooth leaf; or Semi-Savoy, which has less-crinkly leaves than the Savoy. The flat leaf and Semi-Savoy are considered easier to clean than the Savoy types.

Recommended Savoy varieties include 'Bloomsdale', the most commonly grown variety; 'Regiment' (mildew resistant); and 'Samish'.

Flat-leaf varieties include 'Olympia', 'Space' (mildew resistant), 'Red Cardinal', and 'Corvair' (mildew resistant).

Favored Semi-Savory varieties include 'Five Star', 'Tyee' (mildew resistant), 'Catalina', and 'Teton' (mildew resistant).

SQUASH

Easy to love and easy to grow, squash (*Cucurbita pepo*) is the vegetable lover's and vegetable gardener's go-to edible. With so many varieties to

choose from, you can grow a rainbow of squashes in more shapes than you can imagine. All squash is grown to be harvested in summer, but there is summer squash, which is best eaten soon after picking (such as zucchini and crookneck), and there is winter squash, which is harvested in late summer and can keep for several months after picking (such as butternut, delicata, acorn, or pumpkin). Some squash plants are very prolific, and every zucchini grower knows the pressure of the crop that just keeps coming or the squash that didn't get

harvested until it had grown to the size of a watermelon. It's one of the most reliable producers in the vegetable garden, and by following a few simple steps, you can be harvesting more (and more varied) squash than you've ever seen in a grocery store.

When to Plant

Plant squash in the spring when the weather has warmed. In areas with short growing seasons, start seeds indoors a few weeks before the last frost date.

Where to Plant

Squash can be grown throughout California. Plant in full sun in well-drained soil that has been amended with organic matter.

How to Plant

Sow squash seeds 1 inch deep. Bush varieties should be spaced 1½ to 4 feet apart; space vining varieties 5 feet apart. Keep the soil moist; seeds should germinate in seven to ten days.

■ Care and Maintenance

Keep plants evenly watered, preferably with drip irrigation or soaker hoses. Water on foliage and stems creates a welcome environment for disease. Squash plants are heavy feeders, so apply fish emulsion or a balanced fertilizer regularly.

Early in the growing season you should be on the watch for certain pests. Cutworms, cucumber beetles, and slugs can cause considerable damage and should be handpicked. Row covers can help prevent them getting access.

Mildew can be a real problem on squash plants, particularly late in the season. It helps to plant mildew-resistant varieties, but if mildew does become severe, it is sometimes best to just tear out the plant.

■ Harvesting

Summer squash can be harvested in fifty to sixty-five days when the fruits are still tender and the blossoms on the fruit have died back. Be careful not let to them get oversize (which can happen seemingly in the blink of an eye!) because the flavor and the texture start to degrade when they get too big—and production stops! Summer squash can produce as much as one fruit every one to two days.

Harvest winter squash in sixty to one hundred ten days when they are full size and the skin is hard. Cut the squash from the vine, leaving a few inches of stem attached. Keep the squash in a dark, dry, well-ventilated place for two to three weeks to cure, then move them someplace cool

(50° to 60°F) to store them. They will keep for several months. You can expect to get two to six winter squash per vine.

Winter squash is so-called not because it grows during the winter, but because it develops a hard shell and can be stored during the winter. In the case of winter squash (such as pumpkin and butternut), you want the fruits to mature fully so that they store for the longest time possible.

It's more likely that you'll get more squash than you can eat rather than not enough, but if you find that you're getting lots of blossoms but not much fruit, the problem could be that there aren't enough pollinators doing their job. It's easy to hand-pollinate squash. Just take a soft-bristle artist's paintbrush and brush it over the pollen-encrusted stamens of the male blossoms, then carry the pollen over to the female blossoms (which have the immature fruit at the base of the blossom) and brush it over the stigma at the center. You should see an increase in the fruit development.

Additional Information

I love most kinds of squash, but because of the amount of space needed for each plant, I'm usually limited to just a couple plants per year. For those of you with more planting space than I have, here are just some of the delectable varieties to try:

For green zucchini and pattypan squash, check out 'Clarimore' (bush, forty-four days), 'Raven' (bush, forty-eight days), 'Ronde de Nice' (round

fruit, forty-five days), 'Starship' (pattypan, fifty days), 'Peter Pan' (pattypan, fifty days), and 'Romanesco' (striped skin, forty-eight days).

For yellow summer squash, try 'Early Yellow Crookneck' (bush, fifty days), 'Golden Dawn' (forty-seven days), 'Supersett' (crookneck, forty days), 'Sunburst' (pattypan, fifty days), and 'Sunny Delight' (straightneck, semi-bush vine, forty days).

'Tromboncino' is a unique summer squash that grows on a very long vine and produces long-necked fruit up to 24 inches in length in fifty-six days. It looks impressive grown on a pergola so that its pale green fruits can hang down.

Butternut squash is one of my very favorite vegetables. Try 'Burpee's Butterbush' (bush, seventy-five days) or 'Waltham Butternut' (vine, one hundred five days). Other recommended winter squash varieties include 'Buttercup' (vine, ninety-five days), 'Cornell's Bush Delicata' (bush, one hundred days), and 'Sunshine' (vine, ninety-five days).

And don't forget about pumpkins! There are pumpkin varieties with orange or white skin and in every size from miniature (3 to 4 inches) to giant (hundreds of pounds—a recent record-breaker was 1,725 pounds!). Some varieties are favored for soups, some for pies, some for jack-o-lanterns. Sugar pumpkins such as 'Winter Luxury Pie' (one hundred days) and 'Spookie' (ninety days) are good for making pies. French pumpkins such as 'Cinderella's Carriage' (one hundred ten days) and 'Rouge Vif d'Etampes' (one hundred fifteen days), which are flatter and more scalloped than other varieties, are good for soups. For jack-o-lantern carving, try 'Autumn Gold' (one hundred days). And for novelty mini-pumpkins, there's 'Jack-Be-Little' (ninety-five days) and 'Mini Jack' (eighty to eighty-five days). Want to grow a giant? 'Atlantic Giant' (one hundred twenty days) is one of the favorites of the behemoth-growers, but there are also 'Wyatt's Wonder' (one hundred ten days) and 'Big Max' (one hundred twenty days).

Pumpkins have much the same growing requirements as other squash, but they may require more space, depending on the variety. In late summer, slide a piece of wood or some other protection under each pumpkin so that it doesn't rot on the ground. Pumpkins are ready to harvest when the skin is fully colored and hard. Cut the pumpkin from the vine, leaving a couple inches of stem attached.

STRAWBERRY

The first edibles I planted when I got my first house with a garden were strawberries (*Fragaria ananassa*). With my sandy soil, the yield that first year was not exactly spectacular, although each precious berry was more delicious than anything I'd ever tasted from a store. The dream of having lots of plump, pesticide-free berries right outside my back door spurs me on, and each year my strawberry crop does a little better than the year before. I've improved the soil, tried different varieties, and changed the way I water—all for the sake of that little red explosion of flavor. It is so worth the effort!

There are four types of strawberries. The first is spring-bearing (or June-bearing), and it bears mainly in May and June. Next is everbearing, which has a spring crop, that continues producing a few berries throughout summer and has another small crop in late summer into the fall. The third type is day-neutral. It produces a steady harvest from May until frost. The last category is alpine strawberries, tiny, flavorful berries that are hardy in cold regions but don't do well in hot climates.

◼ *When to Plant*

Bare-root strawberries are best planted in spring in cold-winter regions. In mild-winter areas, you can plant in the spring or fall.

◼ *Where to Plant*

You can grow strawberries in Zones 4–11. Plant in full sun in well-draining, slightly acidic soil that's been heavily amended with organic matter. Alpine strawberries should be planted in morning sun or filtered shade. Strawberries cannot tolerate high salt content in the soil, and they are susceptible to verticilium wilt, so do not plant them where tomatoes have grown.

◼ *How to Plant*

Plant bare-root crowns for spring-bearing and everbearing strawberries 6 inches apart in rows 12 inches apart. Day-neutral berries should be spaced 4 to 5 inches apart. Plant so the crown is right at ground level. If you plant them too deep, they may rot; if they're not deep enough, they will dry out. If your soil doesn't have good drainage, build up mounds of soil to plant the crowns in. Water well and mulch. A thick layer of pine needles is an excellent mulch for strawberries since the needles make the soil more acidic.

Alpine strawberries (*Fragaria vesca*) can be grown from seed. Plant indoors in early spring ⅛ inch deep in fine potting soil. Keep the soil evenly moist under a good light source. Germination takes twenty-one to twenty-

eight days. Thin or transplant to 3 inches apart. When seedlings are 3 inches high, begin hardening off and then transplant outdoors, spacing the plants 12 inches apart.

Care and Maintenance

Keep the soil consistently moist but not soggy. Drip irrigation is preferred in order to keep the foliage dry and less hospitable for mildew. In cold-winter areas, mulch heavily with straw.

Apply compost in the spring. Everbearing and day-neutral berries should be fed again once a month for the next two months.

For the first year, remove blossoms from spring-bearing plants. For everbearing plants, remove spring blossoms, but let fall blossoms fruit. For day-neutrals, remove flowers for the first six weeks, then let subsequent flowers develop. Alpines can be left alone to flower and fruit.

Harvesting

At harvest time, you need to check the plants daily because strawberries peak quickly. Pick them when they are fully colored and sweet. Homegrown varieties aren't as firm as store-bought varieties, and they have a very short shelf life. Enjoy them at their best!

Additional Information

Recommended spring-bearing varieties include 'Earliglow', 'Jewel', 'Rainier', 'Sequoia', 'Camarosa', 'Chandler', and 'Pajaro'. For an everbearing crop, try 'Ozark Beauty', 'Quinault', 'Redchief', 'Albion', 'Fort Laramie', and 'Selva'. Good day-neutral varieties for California include 'Seascape', 'Tribute', and 'Tristar'. Gardeners in colder regions may want to plant alpine strawberries; try 'Alexandria', 'Improved Rugen', 'Variegata', and 'Yellow Fruited'.

SWEET POTATO

What would a holiday dinner be without sweet potatoes (*Ipomea batatus*)? Whether you go for that classic miniature marshmallow-topped treatment or some less gooey recipe, sweet potatoes are loved for their sweet, starchy flavor as well as their fiber, beta-carotene, and lack of fat. The sweet potato isn't really a potato at all but a thick root of a tropical vine that is related to the morning glory flower. But that's just a botanical technicality. What really matters is that sweet potatoes are delicious!

When to Plant

Plant sweet potatoes in late spring after danger of frost has passed and the soil temperature has reached 70°F.

Where to Plant

Sweet potatoes can be grown throughout California, but a long, hot growing season is required to produce a good crop. Plant in full sun in well-drained, slightly acidic soil (pH 5.0 to 6.5).

How to Plant

The most important part of planting sweet potatoes is what you plant—use only certified disease-free slips, which are rooted pieces of tuber. You can buy organic sweet potatoes and root them yourself by cutting them in half and placing them on a bed of moist potting soil. Cover with a few inches more of potting soil, and keep them moist and warm until shoots and leaves

appear. In about six weeks, they will be ready to dig up, cut into pieces, and replant. The problem with this is that you must keep the tubers really warm to get the slips started, which usually requires a heating mat or some other heat source. It's just much easier to buy your slips from a trusted seed supplier.

Before planting the slips, apply a fertilizer that is low in nitrogen and high in phosphorus and potassium and work it into the soil several inches deep. Plant the slips so that just the tips of the stems and leaves are exposed. Space them 1 foot apart in rows 3 feet apart. Use ditches between the rows to ensure good drainage.

Keep the bed consistently moist until the plants are established and growing. Once established, the plants require less moisture.

Care and Maintenance

If you added fertilizer to the soil at the time of planting, additional feeding isn't needed and will just increase the foliage without improving the tubers. Using row covers will help keep the bed warmer and will also prevent pests like flea beetles, cucumber beetles, and wireworms from getting access. Nematodes can still be a problem; the best way to combat this is to rotate crops so that you never grow sweet potatoes in the same bed two years in a row.

Harvesting

Most varieties of sweet potato are ready to harvest one hundred ten to one hundred twenty days after planting. You should harvest before the first frost; if a sudden frost should kill the plants, harvest the tubers immediately.

To harvest, dig carefully with a garden fork or shovel. Dry the roots in the sun until they are dry enough to brush the dirt off. They then need to be cured someplace that is warm (at least 85°F) and humid for ten to fourteen days before storing in a cool, dry place (not below 55°F). The flavor will improve with storage.

Additional Information

There are two kinds of sweet potatoes—those with sweet, orange-yellow flesh and those with firmer, dryer white flesh. The orange-flesh type is the kind you see sold in supermarkets as yams. Recommended varieties of this type include 'Centennial', 'Jewel', 'Kona-B', 'Vineless Puerto Rico', 'Nancy Hall', and 'Vardaman'. Favored white-flesh varieties include 'Onokeo', 'Waimanalo Red', and 'Yellow Jersey'.

SWISS CHARD

Swiss chard is one of my favorite edibles, both on the plate and in the garden. A relative of the beet, Swiss chard (*Beta vulgaris chicla*) is grown for its nutrient-rich leaves and stalks, loaded with vitamins A, C, E, and K, plus fiber, magnesium, manganese, and potassium. It's a great-looking plant besides, especially in its more colorful forms. It is a beautiful accent in a flower bed and so, so easy to grow. It's also easy to eat. The greens are great in a salad, or cooked along with the stems in a sauté. They can be used in egg dishes and casseroles, but my very favorite way to eat chard is to simply chop it up and toss it in a pan of hot chicken broth with some tortellini for a simple and delicious soup. Painless to grow and painless to prepare—that's my kind of vegetable!

When to Plant

The best planting time for chard is spring to early summer. In mild-winter areas it can also be planted in late summer and fall for harvest into winter.

Where to Plant

You can grow Swiss chard throughout California. Plant in full sun or in partial shade in the hottest regions. It prefers cool, mild conditions and can tolerate light frosts. It also does well as a container plant.

How to Plant

Start seeds indoors or direct-seed outdoors. Work compost into the soil before planting, then sow seeds ½ inch deep and 2 inches apart in rows 10 inches apart. You can also broadcast seeds over a bed. Tamp soil down firmly over seeds to make sure they make good contact with the soil. Apply a fish emulsion solution and keep the bed evenly moist. Seeds should germinate in five to seven days. When seedlings are 2 to 3 inches high, thin plants to 1 foot apart. Use the thinnings as you would any baby greens.

Care and Maintenance

As the chard grows, mulch the area and keep it weeded. Apply more fish emulsion six weeks after planting and again a month later. In areas where you can grow chard through winter, do not fertilize when soil temperature is below 40°F.

Harvesting

Chard is usually ready to begin harvesting about fifty days after planting. You can either cut the entire plant at the ground, or cut outer leaves, leaving the inner leaves to grow. New leaves will grow in at the center and the plant will keep producing until the winter. In my Bay Area garden where the winters are mild, I've had chard grow for well over a year.

Additional Information

Swiss chard is available in the classic white-stemmed varieties as well as shades of deep red, golden yellow, and vivid orange. If there is a difference in taste between the white and the colored stems, I have not been able to discern it. Aside from the color of the stem, and in some cases the darkness of the green leaves, the main difference is that the white-stemmed varieties often have wide stems. The favored white-stemmed varieties include 'Barese', 'Fordhook Giant', 'French Swiss', and 'Italian Silver Rib'. Colored-rib varieties include 'Bright Yellow', 'Golden Sunrise', 'Rhubarb', 'Ruby', 'Scarlet Charlotte', 'Pot of Gold', and the rainbow mixes 'Bright Lights', 'Rainbow', and 'Neon Glow'.

THYME

Thyme (*Thymus vulgaris*) is one of my very favorite herbs, both in cooking and in the garden. An aromatic evergreen perennial running from 2 to 15 inches in height, thyme can be used as a shrub or a groundcover, and its foliage comes in lush shades of gray-green, dark green, or even silver or gold. It produces lavender, white, or pink flowers that the bees love and is a big help in attracting pollinators to your garden. In addition to its use as a food seasoning, thyme has long had homeopathic and traditional uses ranging from an embalming agent to a sleep aid, and in ancient times it was considered a source of courage to those who carried sprigs of its leaves.

When to Plant

Plant thyme from seed in late winter to early spring in order for plants to be harvested from spring through fall.

Where to Plant

Thyme is a frost-hardy perennial that can be grown in Zones 3–10. Plant in full sun or in light shade in the hottest climates. It needs excellent drainage and actually prefers rocky or sandy soil. It makes a nice mounding or cascading addition to a container, and the creeping varieties can be used as a groundcover or filler around steppingstones or in flagstone paths and patios.

How to Plant

It is best to start seeds indoors in late winter, sowing seeds ⅛ inch deep and covering very thinly with potting soil or vermiculite. Tamp down to make

sure the seeds are making good contact with the soil and keep the soil evenly moist with a good light source. Seeds should germinate in fourteen to twenty-one days. You can also direct-seed thyme outdoors when the soil can be worked. Seedlings should be thinned or transplanted to 10 to 12 inches apart.

■ Care and Maintenance

Thyme is fairly drought-tolerant once established, but in very hot climates it will need supplemental water. Prune the plant back after blossoms have faded or in the spring to encourage new growth and to keep its compact shape.

■ Harvesting

Once the plant is established, thyme can be harvested at any time. If gathering leaves to dry, it is best to take them just before the bloom period. Thyme can also be frozen.

■ Additional Information

There is quite a range of forms, fragrances, and flavors of thyme. Plant an entire bed of thyme and you will have a real sensory showcase. Here are some of the favorite types:

Common thyme, English thyme, and French thyme grow from 6 to 18 inches high and have gray leaves with lavender flowers.

Creeping thyme is a groundcover growing to only 2 to 4 inches in height. It is dark green with purple, rose, and white flowers. It has a bland flavor, and although it is edible, it is not generally used for food.

Citrus thymes include lemon, lime, and silver thyme. Lime thyme has lime green leaves and lime flavor. Silver thyme is basically a variegated silver/green version of lemon thyme. There is also a creeping form of lemon thyme with gold variegated leaves, pink flowers, and lemon scent and flavor.

Caraway thyme is a groundcover form with a strong caraway scent. Woolly thyme is also a groundcover, but it is not used for culinary purposes.

TOMATO

I love growing tomatoes (*Lycopersicon esculentum*). I love the aroma of the bright green leaves. I love the ease with which the seeds germinate and grow. I love the look of the lush plants, the delicate yellow blossoms, and the bright colors of the red, orange, yellow, green, or purple fruit. As a matter of fact, I love everything about tomatoes—except the taste. The most common reason why people begin to grow vegetables is because they are dying for the full flavor of a homegrown tomato. But the thought of biting into a fresh, raw tomato makes me shudder. Yes, I know they're really good for you, being high in vitamins A and C, antioxidants, and fiber. For me, however, tomatoes are a giveaway crop, and I'm happy to pass them on to others. Growing them is pleasure enough for me.

When to Plant

Start seeds indoors six to eight weeks before the average last spring frost date. Seedlings can be planted outdoors as soon as all danger of frost has passed and nighttime temperatures are consistently above 50°F.

Where to Plant

Tomatoes can be grown throughout California, but finding the variety best suited for your climate is key. Plant in full sun (six hours minimum per day) in well-drained soil that is rich in organic matter.

How to Plant

Sow seeds ¼ inch deep and 1 inch apart in flats of sterile potting soil. Keep seeds evenly moist and warm (75° to 80°F) and under a good light source. Seeds should germinate in seven to fourteen days. When seedlings develop their true leaves (the second leaf set), transplant to individual pots, burying

the stems up to the bottom leaves. Planting them this deeply will help them develop more roots. Feed with a half-strength fish emulsion solution or other liquid fertilizer every two weeks until they are ready to harden off and transplant outdoors.

Once the seedlings are hardened off, work compost into the bed and plant the tomatoes 2 to 3 feet apart, again burying the stems up to the bottom leaves. If plants are leggy, you can bury them even deeper—more roots will develop along the buried stem and the plant will be fuller and stronger.

■ Care and Maintenance

Provide about an inch of water per week, more in extremely hot weather. Drip irrigation is best, as overhead watering can spread disease and uneven watering can contribute to blossom end rot disease. Mulching also helps control the moisture conditions and helps suppress weeds as well. Some people feel that cutting back on the amount of water for a week or so before fruit is harvested results in better-tasting tomatoes.

Make sure that plants have sufficient support with stakes or wire cages. Otherwise, branches will break off and you'll lose fruit before it's ripe. It's best to set up the support at the time of planting. I recommend that you not bother with the funnel-shaped wire tomato supports that are commonly sold in hardware stores and garden center. Except for the smallest tomato plants, they provide completely inadequate support and are a waste of money.

When blossoms set, fertilize with a fish emulsion solution every month. As more blossoms and fruit set, prune out non-fruit-bearing branches to increase the air circulation around the plant and to channel the plant's energy to developing fruit. You can continue this periodic pruning throughout the growing season.

Tomatoes are susceptible to a long list of pests, including tomato hornworms, whiteflies, cutworms, tobacco budworms, flea beetles, and gophers. Of even greater concern is the list of diseases that can plague tomato plants: verticilium wilt, fusarium wilt, rootknot nematodes, alternaria, late blight, and tomato mosaic virus. Some of these diseases, such as verticilium and fusarium, are particularly troubling because they not only kill your tomato plants, they also live in the soil, sometimes for many years, and will kill any subsequent plantings that are vulnerable to them. Planting disease-resistant varieties will lessen the chance of infection, but it's no guarantee. Rotating crops from year to year can lessen the risk of infection.

■ *Harvesting*

Tomatoes are ready to harvest they're when fully colored and slightly soft to the touch. If there are still green tomatoes on the vines at the end of the season, you can cut off the branches with fruit and hang them somewhere cool and dark to finish ripening. A healthy plant can yield between 20 to 30 pounds of tomatoes.

■ *Additional Information*

When selecting tomato varieties, in addition to climate concerns, you should also pay attention to whether the plants are determinate or indeterminate. Determinate varieties are bushier, more limited in height, and can usually get by without staking or other support. Indeterminate varieties are more like vines and grow to 6 or 7 feet with the proper support. Indeterminate plants are typically more productive, bearing over a longer period of time.

For areas with cool or short growing seasons, recommended varieties include 'San Francisco Fog', 'Early Girl', 'Fourth of July', 'Siberia', 'Stupice', 'Gold Nugget', 'Legend', 'Oregon Spring', 'Oregon Pride', and 'Siletz'. Smaller tomatoes (cherry, grape, or currant) tend to do well in cooler areas as well. Some of the favorites of the small tomatoes include 'Sun Gold', 'Supersweet 100', 'Sweet 100', 'Sweet Million', and 'Juliet'.

In hot-summer areas, try 'Creole', 'Eva Purple Ball', 'Ozark Pink', 'Solar Set', 'Tropic', and 'Viva Italia'. Large beefsteak tomatoes do better in these regions as well; recommended hybrids include 'Beefsteak', 'Beefmaster', 'Big Beef', and 'Delicious'.

Heirloom varieties gain more and more fans every year, but they do have some challenges in terms of their susceptibility to disease. But for tomato lovers, the flavor of heirlooms is worth the risk. Some favorite heirloom varieties include 'Brandywine', 'Mortgage Lifter', 'Green Zebra', 'Black Krim', 'Cherokee Purple', 'Marvel Stripe', and 'Principe Borghese'.

TURNIP

If you enjoy getting double the reward for your gardening efforts, turnips (*Brassica rapa* var. *rapifera*) and their close relatives, rutabagas, may be the crops for you. Just like other members of the cabbage family, turnips and rutabagas are cool-season crops, meaning in some areas you can get both an early crop and a second crop later in the year. Plus, turnips give you two harvests in one because you can be clipping off the turnip greens to eat while the edible roots are still growing. While some people aren't crazy about the flavor of turnips, it's helpful to keep in mind that the amount of water the roots get directly affects its flavor. The drier the growing conditions, the more pungent the flavor.

▦ When to Plant

In cold-winter areas, plant in early spring for harvest in early summer or in summer for harvest in fall. In mild-winter areas, plant in fall for a winter crop.

▦ Where to Plant

Turnips and rutabagas can be grown in all zones. Plant in full sun in well-drained soil that's high in organic matter. It prefers acidic soil, but can tolerate slightly alkaline soil (pH 6.0 to 7.5).

▦ How to Plant

Like most root crops, turnips and rutabagas require loose, well-worked soil; rocks and hard clumps can deform and stunt the roots. Once the soil is prepared, sow seeds ¼ to ½ inch deep, 1 inch apart in rows 12 to 18 inches apart. Seeds germinate in four to seven days. When seedlings reach a couple of inches high, thin turnips to 4 to 6 inches apart and rutabagas to 5 to 8 inches apart.

▦ Care and Maintenance

Ample, consistent water is essential for turnips and rutabagas. The moister the soil, the milder the flavor of the roots. Both vegetables may be affected by root maggots and other pests attracted to Brassica plants. Keep watch for any appearance of caterpillars on the plants. Pick them off and apply B.t. (*Bacillus thuringiensis*) to control an infestation. Floating row covers can also be used to prevent infestation. To help control pest and disease problems, do not plant any crops in the Brassica family (broccoli, cabbage, kale, cauliflower) in the same spot in consecutive years.

▦ *Harvesting*

Turnip greens can be harvested before the roots mature. Cut the outer leaves first but be sure to leave some leaves behind to keep the root growth going. Roots should be harvested when they reach 2 to 3 inches wide, about fifty to seventy-five days after sowing. Leaving them in the ground beyond this point may make them tougher or woodier. Use a garden fork or shovel to dig up the roots, brush off the dirt and twist off the greens, leaving about a ½ inch of stem. Do not wash the turnips if you plan on storing them. They can be stored in a cool, dark place for up to three months.

Rutabagas are slower growers and may require ninety to one hundred twenty days to mature. Harvest the roots when they reach 3 inches wide. Rutabagas can be stored for up to four months, or stored in the ground during winter. Light frosts will improve their flavor.

▦ *Additional Information*

Recommended varieties of turnips include 'Purple Top White Globe', 'Tokyo Cross Hybrid', and 'Shogoin'. 'American Purple Top' is the most recommended variety of rutabaga.

GLOSSARY

Acid soil: Soil that measures between 0 to 7 on the pH scale.

Alkaline soil: Soil that measures between 7 to 14 on the pH scale.

Annual: A plant that lives its entire life cyle in one growing season.

Biennial: A plant that establishes itself in the first year, then flowers and sets seed before dying in the second year.

Blanching: Wrapping a plant, such as cauliflower, as it's growing to block the production of chlorophyll so that the plant turns white.

Bolting: Setting seed; sometimes caused by warmer temperatures.

Broadcasting: Sowing seed by sprinkling it broadly over a prepared bed.

B.t.: *Bacillus thuringiensis*; a bacterium commonly used as a biological pesticide.

Bulb: A shortened, modified underground stem with fleshy leaves that contains stored nutrition for the plant contained within. Onions and garlic are examples of bulbs.

Central leader: One central trunk of a tree. Some trees naturally have a central leader; others can be trained to have a central leader.

Chill hours: The number of hours that a tree must spend below 45°F to blossom and set fruit. The hours can be cumulative, but it is preferable that they occur in December and January.

Clay soil: A soil type made up of very fine particles that tend to hold together when compressed. Clay soil holds water and nutrients longer than sandy soil, but easily becomes waterlogged when wet and very hard when dry.

Companion planting: A long-practiced method of closely planting different plants that mutually benefit each other. The plants may help each other manage pests, uptake nutrition, and increase pollination.

Compost: Organic matter that has decomposed and is used as an organic fertilizer or mulch.

Composted manure: Animal manure (usually steer, chicken, or rabbit) that has decomposed and is used as an organic fertilizer.

Crop rotation: The practice of moving crops from one space to another so they are not planted in the same spot in consecutive years to avoid pest infestations and soil deficiencies.

Cutworm: Moth larvae that reside in the soil and come out at night to feed, cutting stems down at soil level.

Damping off: Any type of fungal disease that attacks young seedlings and kills them.

Deciduous: Refers to trees, shrubs, or herbaceous perennials that lose their leaves at some point in the season. Most deciduous plants in California lose their leaves in winter; some California native plants are summer deciduous.

Direct-seed: Sowing seeds directly in the ground outside rather than starting seeds indoors to transplant.

Dormant: A period in a plant's life cycle when its growth temporarily comes to a stop, usually triggered by environmental conditions such as temperature or light.

Drainage: The passage of water through soil.

Drip line: The perimeter around the area that is covered by the entire canopy of a tree.

Drought: An extended period (months or years) when a region experiences a shortage in its water supply, usually due to less than normal rainfall.

Espalier: The practice of pruning and training trees into relatively flat forms, often against a wall or fence. Espaliers can be formal or informal and can be used as a small-space gardening technique.

Fertilizer: Organic or inorganic material that is added to soil or sprayed on plants to supply one or more nutrients.

Fish emulsion: An organic fertilizer made from the liquid remains of fish, typically having an N-P-K rating of 5-2-2.

Foliar feeding: Applying a liquid fertilizer solution that is sprayed onto the foliage of plants so it can be absorbed by the leaves.

Full sun: Six or more hours of sunlight each day.

Fungicide: Chemical or biological controls used to kill fungi and fungal spores that can attack plants.

Germination: The process whereby a plant emerges from a seed and begins to grow.

Graft union: The place on a tree or shrub where the scion of one plant is grafted onto the rootstock of another plant and the two plants grow together.

Hardening off: The process of acclimating seedlings that have been started indoors to outdoor conditions over a period of time.

Heirloom plants: Cultivars that were commonly grown in the past but are not currently grown in commercial agriculture, often because they do not ship or store well. Many heirloom edibles are becoming popular again with home growers.

Humus: Organic matter that has broken down completely, used to enrich soil.

Hybrid: A cross of two genetically different plants. Hybrids can occur naturally or by intentionally cross-breeding two plants to achieve a desired combination of characteristics.

Inorganic: Not involving living organisms or the products of their life processes.

Insecticide: Any compound, organic or synthetic, used to kill or control populations of insects.

Integrated pest management: An integrated method of crop management aimed at controlling pest populations with little or no use of pesticides.

Interplanting: Mixed planting of fast-growing and slow-growing plants to maximize available space. Can also refer to mixed planting of edible and ornamental plants.

Irrigation: Various methods of bringing water to plants.

Larva: The juvenile, wormlike form of insects before undergoing metamorphosis into their adult form.

Leaf beetles: The large family of beetles that feed on plant tissue. Examples include asparagus beetles, cucumber beetles, and flea beetles.

Leafminers: Insect larvae that live in and eat the leaf tissue of plants. Leafminers can be difficult to control because they are protected from predators by living within the leaf tissue.

Lime: Pulverized limestone that is added to soil to raise the pH level to make the soil less acidic.

Loam: Soil that is composed of sand, silt, and clay in proportions (roughly 40–40–20) that make it desirable for growing most plants.

Maggot: The larva of a fly, which can bore into and live off of ripe fruit.

Manure: Animal or plant waste that is used as organic fertilizer.

Micronutrients: Nutrients that are needed in very small quantities for plants to sustain life and grow. The seven essential micronutrients for plants are manganese, boron, copper, iron, chlorine, molybdenum, and zinc.

Mildew: Certain kinds of molds or fungi. The most common kinds of mildew on plants are powdery mildew and downy mildew.

Mites: Tiny, often microscopic, parasitic arthropods. Some of the mites most troubling for plants are spider mites and gall mites.

Mold: Fungal spores that grow on plant tissue. Some of the more problematic molds include sooty mold and gray mold.

Mulch: A layer of material spread over soil to retain moisture, reduce erosion, and suppress weeds. Mulches can be organic, such as wood chips, compost, newspaper, or cardboard, or inorganic, such as plastic or rubber.

Neem oil: An organic pesticide derived from the seed of the Neem tree. This oil deters a large number of insects, including Japanese beetles, from feeding and reproducing.

Nematodes: Microscopic worms that live in soil. Nematodes can be beneficial or parasitic.

Nitrogen: One of the three main nutrients needed by plants. Nitrogen, which is represented by N in the N-P-K analysis of fertilizer nutrients, encourages green growth in plants.

N-P-K: The analysis of nutrients used on fertilizer labeling. N stands for nitrogen, P stands for phosphorus, and K stands for potassium—the three major plant nutrients.

Organic gardening: Gardening using biological controls and methods to manage pests, improve soil, and encourage plant growth while excluding the use of synthetic pesticides and fertilizers that can be toxic and damaging to the environment and other living organisms.

Organic matter: Material derived from decaying or decayed animals or plants, used to improve soil quality and deliver nutrients to plants.

Peat: Partially decayed vegetation that forms in bogs and is used to amend soil to improve its structure and increase its acidity. Peat is not considered to be a sustainable product, so its use is discouraged. Sphagnum peat is decayed peat moss and is considered by some to be more sustainable, although this is somewhat in dispute.

Perennial: A plant whose life cycle spans more than one year or growing season. Herbaceous perennials will die back to the ground at the end of each growing season but resprout from the same root system the following year.

pH: The measurement of the acidity or alkalinity. pH level affects how nutrients are available to plants.

Phosphorus: One of the three main nutrients needed by plants. Phosphorus, which is represented by P in the N-P-K analysis of fertilizer nutrients, encourages bloom and fruiting in plants.

Pinching: Removing the new tips of plants to encourage new growth further down the plant; a method to improve the fullness and bushiness of plants.

Potassium: One of the three main nutrients needed by plants. Potassium, which is represented by K in the N-P-K analysis of fertilizer nutrients, encourages overall vigor in plants.

Powdery mildew: A fungal disease that appears on plants, looking as though the leaves have been dusted with powder. Powdery mildew will usually not kill a plant, but it will inhibit its ability to photosynthesize.

Pyrethrum: An organic insecticide made from chrysanthemum flowers.

Raised bed: A method of building soil up above the ground within a contained area for planting. Raised beds can be used when the existing soil is deficient, contaminated, or otherwise inadequate for growing, or they can be used to increase accessibility for the gardener.

Rootball: The mass of soil and roots that is usually enclosed in a burlap sack or plastic nursery pot in a tree or shrub purchased from a garden center.

Rootbound: When a plant has grown too large for its container, resulting in matting or tangling of the roots.

Rootstock: A plant with a healthy root system that is used to graft a desired plant variety onto. Rootstocks are usually selected for disease resistance or dwarfing characteristics.

Rototill: To turn over the soil using a special machine with metal tines. While rototilling is often used to create a garden bed in spring, too much tilling can cause harm to the soil structure.

Sandy soil: Soil with a high percentage of sand particles. Sandy soils are fast-draining, which can make it more difficult for plants to absorb nutrients.

Seedling: An immature plant, usually grown from seed.

Side-dress: The technique of applying fertilizer or compost in a row a couple inches from the plant stems.

Soil test: Tests to measure nutrients, pH level, heavy metals, and more in soil samples. Tests can be purchased to run at home or sent to a lab.

Soluble fertilizer: Fertilizers that can be dissolved in water. Soluble fertilizers can be easily applied to soil, but they also quickly leach out of well-draining soils.

Spur: Short (3- to 5-inch) woody branches that bear blossoms and fruit on some fruit trees.

Stone fruit: Fruits with an outer fleshy part surrounding a hard pit with seed inside.

Succession planting: Planting the same crop in repeat cycles at fixed intervals in order to prolong the harvest.

Tendril: A modified stem or leaf with a threadlike shape that climbing plants use for support.

Thinning: Removing some plants, usually as young seedlings, to allow more room for the remaining plants to grow.

Topsoil: The upper layer of soil, usually just a few inches deep, containing organic matter, microorganisms, and nutrients to support plant growth.

Trace elements: Chemical elements that are required in minute quantities for a plant to achieve proper growth. Also called *micronutrients*.

Transplant: Moving a plant from one container or location to another.

True leaves: Leaves that form after the first set of leaves following seed germination. While the first set of leaves of all plants generally look more or less alike, the true leaves will have the shape and appearance of the leaves of the mature plant.

Tuber: Modified stems or roots that are enlarged to store nutrients. Potatoes are an example of a stem tuber; sweet potatoes are an example of a root tuber.

Viability: The ability of a plant to grow and thrive.

Virus: A microorganism that infects and can potentially kill plants. Viruses are usually spread to plants by sucking insects such as aphids.

Wireworms: The larvae of certain beetles that attack root crops such as carrots, beets, and potatoes.

RESOURCES

Seeds

The following seed companies offer a great selection of hybrid and heirloom seeds for edibles.

Baker Creek Heirloom Seeds
www.rareseeds.com
2278 Baker Creek Rd.
Mansfield, MO 65704
Phone: 417-924-8917
Fax: 417-924-8887

Baker Creek Petaluma Seed Bank
199 Petaluma Blvd. North
Petaluma, CA 94952
Phone: 707-509-5171

Kitazawa Seed Co.
www.kitazawaseed.com
PO Box 13220
Oakland, CA 94661-3220
Phone: 510-595-1188
Fax: 510-595-1860

Renee's Garden Seeds
www.reneesgarden.com
6060A Graham Hill Rd.
Felton, CA 95018
Phone: 888-880-7228

Seeds from Italy
www.growitalian.com
PO Box 3908
Lawrence, KS 66046
Phone: 785-748-0959

Sustainable Seed Co.
www.sustainableseedco.com
Phone: 877-620-SEED

Nurseries

When local nurseries don't have the varieties you need, check out these mail-order nurseries for a wide selection of vegetables and fruit trees.

Annie's Annuals
www.anniesannuals.com
801 Chesley Ave.
Richmond, CA 94801
Phone: 888-266-4370

Four Winds Growers
www.fourwindsgrowers.com
Phone: 877-449-4637, ext. 1

One Green World
www.onegreenworld.com
28696 S. Cramer Rd.
Molalla, OR 97038-8576
Phone: 877-353-4028

Networks & Information

Ample Harvest
www.ampleharvest.org

This is a national organization that works to connect home gardeners with local food pantries that can use their surplus crops. Just plug in your zip code and it gives you contact information for participating food banks near you.

California Rare Fruit Growers
www.crfg.org

This organization's website is a treasure-trove of information on growing fruit in California. Check out the local chapter events in your area and meet the CRFG members—they're some of the most knowledgeable gardeners you'll ever meet.

The Edible Schoolyard Project
www.edibleschoolyard.org

This non-profit organization supports the development of edible gardens in schools and food curriculums.

Plant Maps
www.plantmaps.com/index.php

Plug in your zip code on this site, and it will show you not only your USDA hardiness zone, but also first and last average frost dates, minimum and maximum monthly temperatures, and average monthly precipitation.

Slow Food USA
www.slowfoodusa.org

Slow Food is a growing global grassroots movement dedicated to reversing the effects of fast food and rebuilding people's relationship with food, food growing, and the environment.

FOR FURTHER READING

There are many helpful gardening books out there, but here are a few I've found to be particularly informative, helpful, and inspirational.

All New Square Foot Gardening
by Mel Bartholomew
Cool Springs Press, 2006

Bartholomew's book is the bible for gardeners who want to squeeze every bit of productivity out of every square foot of their gardens.

The Complete Idiot's Guide to Composting
by Chris McLaughlin
Alpha, 2010

Great vegetable gardens need great soil, and compost is soil's best friend. McLaughlin's book will tell you everything you need to know to turn your garden and kitchen waste into healthy compost.

The Edible Front Yard: The Mow-Less, Grow-More Plan for a Beautiful, Bountiful Garden
by Ivette Soler
Timber Press, 2011

Soler enthusiastically presents ideas and practices for mixing edible and ornamental plants in the front yard while maintaining curb appeal.

Edible Landscaping
by Rosalind Creasy
Sierra Club Books, 2010

I consider Creasy, who lives and gardens in California, one of the true authorities on growing edibles. Any of her books are useful, but this book is so packed full of ideas for creating beautiful and productive edibles gardens that I would recommend it to every home gardener.

Gardening at the Dragon's Gate: At Work in the Wild and Cultivated World
by Wendy Johnson
Bantam Dell, 2008

Drawing on her years of gardening at the Green Gulch Farm Zen Center in Marin County, California, Johnson has created a book loaded with gardening stories, packed with information, and laced with recipes, practical advice, and other grace notes.

Garden Up! Smart Vertical Gardening for Small and Large Spaces
by Susan Morrison and Rebecca Sweet
Cool Springs Press, 2011

Although this book doesn't focus entirely on edible gardens, Morrison and Sweet present lots of great ideas for optimizing your garden space with vertical gardening techniques.

The Small Budget Gardener
by Maureen Gilmer
Cool Springs Press, 2009

This book will more than pay for itself with all the tips it provides for cutting all kinds of gardening costs. For gardeners who are growing edibles in order to reduce their food budget, this book can help improve their bottom line.

In addition, there are a few magazines that are extremely helpful for anyone growing edibles:

Mother Earth News
www.motherearthnews.com

Organic Gardening
www.organicgardening.com

Urban Farm
www.urbanfarmonline.com

PHOTOGRAPHY CREDITS

Cool Springs Press would like to thank the following contributors to *California Fruit & Vegetable Gardening*:

Front Cover Main Image
Tomatoes (*Lycopersicon esculentum*), www.Thinkstock.com

Cover Photography Provided by Tom Eltzroth
Watermelon (*Citrullus lanatus*), Strawberries (*Fragaria ananassa*), Blueberries (*Vaccinnium ashei*), Potatoes (*Solanum tuberosum*), Carrots (*Daucus carota*), Corn (*Zea mays*), Oranges (*Citrus sinensis*), Cabbage (*Brassica oleracea*), and Onions (*Allium cepa*).

Interior Photography
Cathy Barash: 55; Claire Splan: 108, 120, 134, 145, 149, 152, 160, 163, 168, 170, 174, 181, 195, 213, 219; Dave Wilson Nursery: 190; Ed Rode: 25, 86, 95; Felder Rushing: 64b; Greg Grant: 10, 12, 14, 15, 16, 17, 18–19, 20, 31, 32, 39, 41, 48, 53b, 57b, 60, 76, 77, 107, 110, 138, 183; Joe Lamp'l: 29; Joe Lamp'l and Courtenay Vanderbilt: 65; Jerry Pavia: 197; Lorenzo Gunn: 90, 91, 94, 186, 194; Liz Ball: 191; Mary Ann Newcomer: 185; Maureen Gilmer: 53a; Paul Moore: 22, 28, 30; Monrovia: 96; Neil Soderstrom: 11, 13, 36, 37, 38, 42, 43, 44, 45, 47, 49, 50, 51, 52, 56, 57a, 63, 64a, 67, 85; Robert Bowden & Leu Gardens: 21, 46, 61, 62, 66a, 66b, 66c; Tom Eltzroth: 89, 93, 99, 100, 103, 104, 105, 106, 111, 112, 113, 114, 116, 119, 123, 124, 127, 129, 130, 132, 133, 135, 136, 137, 141, 142, 146, 150, 156, 159, 161, 162, 164, 167, 169, 173, 177, 182, 188, 189, 192, 198, 202, 205, 206, 208, 209, 210, 214, 216, 218, 220, 221, 225; USDA Aphis Division: 68; iStockphoto.com/foued42: 34; iStockphoto.com/Ogphoto: 151; iStockphoto.com/motorolka: 157; iStockphoto.com/Serge Kashkin: 178; Comstock Images/ Jupiter Images: 5; Jupiter Images: 8, 35, 54, 59, 222; AlexTois/ Shutterstock.com: 155; Murat Besler/Shutterstock.com: 201

SPRING

SUMMER

SUMMER

FALL

WINTER

INDEX

Abelmoschus esculentus, 168–69
Actinidia arguta, 154–55
Allium ampeloprasum, 158–59
Allium cepa, 172–73
Allium sativum, 146–47
almonds, 88–89
alpine strawberries, 212–13
AmpleHarvest.org, 18
anthracnose, 78
aphids, 69
Apium graveolens rapaceum, 126–27
Apium graveolens var. *dulce*, 126–27
apples, 90–93
apricots, 94–95
apriums, 195
Arbor Day Foundation, 27
    See also cold-hardiness zones
artichokes, 96–97
arugula, 162–63
Asian pears, 184–85
asparagus, 98–99
Asparagus officinalis, 98–99
avocados, 100–101

Bacillus thuringiensis, 68
Baker Creek Heirloom Seeds, 26
bananas, 102–3
Bartholomew, Mel, 28
basil, 104–5
beans, 106–9
beetles, 69
beets, 110–11
beneficial bugs, 63–65
Beta vulgaris, 110–11
Beta vulgaris chicla, 216–17
blackberries, 114–15
blueberries, 112–13
botrytis, 78–79
brambleberries, 114–15
Brassica oleracea, 116–17, 124–25
Brassica oleracea var. *acephala*, 152–53
Brassica oleracea var. *capitata*, 120–21
Brassica oleracea var. *gemmifera*, 118–19
Brassica oleracea var. *gongylodes*, 156–57

Brassica rapa, 116–17
Brassica rapa var. *rapifera*, 224–25
broad beans, 106–9
broadcasting seeds, 27–28
broccoli, 116–17
broccoli raab, 116–17
Brussels sprouts, 118–19
bugs
    beneficial, 63–65
    common pests, 68–75
    pest controls, 65–66
    pesticides, 66–68
    by plant, 70–75
    types of, 62–65

cabbage, 120–21
California climate, 11–13
California Rare Fruit Growers, 31
cantaloupes, 166–67
Capsicum spp., 188–89
carrots, 122–23
Carya illinoensis, 186–87
cauliflower, 124–25
celeriac, 126–27
celery, 126–27
chemical pesticides, 67–68
cherries, 128–29
chickory, 163
chill hours, 26–27
Cichorium endivia, 163
Cichorium endivia var. *crispum*, 163
Cichorium intybus, 163
cilantro, 130–31
Citrullus lanatus var. *lanatus*, 166–67
Citrus spp., 132–35
citrus trees, 132–35
city ordinances, 21
cold-hardiness zones, 8–9, 12, 26–27
container gardening, 31–32
coriander, 130–31
Coriandrum sativum, 130–31
corn, 136–39
Creasy, Rosilind, 17
cucumbers, 140–41
Cucumis melo, 166–67

Cucumis sativum, 140–41
Cucurbita pepo, 208–11
cutworms, 69
Cydonia oblonga, 200–201
Cynara scolymus, 96–97

Daucus carota, 122–23
Diospyros kaki, 190–91
direct sowing, 34–38
diseases
    common diseases, 78–84
    by plant, 80–84
    spraying for, 84–85
    types of, 76–78
double-digging soil, 43
drainage, 20–21, 43–44
dry beans, 106–9
dwarf trees, 31

edible flowers, 24
eggplants, 142–43
endive, 163
Environmental Working Group, 23
Eriobotrya japonica, 164–65
Eruca sativa, 162–63
escarole, 163
exercise, 17
Extension offices, 19

Feijoa sellowiana, 192–93
fertilizers, 46–48
Ficus carica, 144–45
figs, 144–45
fireblight, 79
flavor of vegetables, 16
food contamination, 17
Fragaria ananassa, 212–13
Fragaria vesca, 212–13
frisée, 163
frost dates, 33
fusarium wilt, 79

Gardener's Supply Company, 26
garden journals, 18
garden location, 20–21

garden mapping, 26
garden size, 22–23
garden tools, 55–59
Garden Writers Association, 16
garlic, 146–47
grapefruits, 132–35
grapes, 148–49
guavas, 150–51

hardening off, 39
heirloom varietals, 16–17, 25–26, 41
high-density planting, 31
homeowner association bylaws, 21
honeydews, 166–67
horticultural oils, 67
hydrozoning, 52

insecticidal soaps, 67–68
insects, *See* bugs
integrated pest management (IPM), 63
interplanting, 30
Ipomea batatus, 214–15
irrigation, 21, 50–54

kale, 152–53
kiwis, 154–55
kohlrabi, 156–57
kumquats, 132–35

Lactuca spp., 160–63
leeks, 158–59
lemons, 132–35
lettuce, 160–63
lima beans, 106–9
limes, 132–35
loquats, 164–65
Lycopersicon esculentum, 220–23

mache, 163
Malus domestica, 90–93
mandarin oranges, 132–35
mealybugs, 70
melons, 166–67
mildew, 79
mites, 70

mosaic virus, 79
mulch, 52
Musa acuminata, 102–3
muskmelons, 166–67
Mycobacterium vaccae, 17–18

nectarines, 182–83
Neem, 66–67
nematodes, 46
neonicotinoids, 68
nitrogen levels, 46, 46–47

Ocimum basilicum, 104–5
okra, 168–69
Olea europaea, 170–71
olive trees, 170–71
onions, 172–73

parsley, 174–75
parsnips, 176–77
Passiflora edulis, 178–79
passion fruit, 178–79
Pastinaca sativa, 176–77
peaches, 182–83
pears, 184–85
peas, 180–81
pecans, 186–87
peppers, 188–89
Persea americana, 100–101
persimmons, 190–91
pest controls, 65–66
pesticides, 66–68
Petroselinum crispum, 174–75
Phaseolus coccineus, 106–9
Phaseolus lunatus, 106–9
Phaseolus vulgaris, 106–9
pH levels, 12, 45
phosphorus levels, 47
pineapple guavas, 192–93
Pisum sativum, 180–81
plant-derived pesticides, 66–67
planting timing, 32–33
plant rotation, 13
plumcots, 195
plums, 194–95

pluots, 195
pomegranates, 196–97
potassium levels, 47
potatoes, 198–99
Prunus armeniaca, 94–95
Prunus avium, 128–29
Prunus domestica, 194–95
Prunus dulcis, 88–89
Prunus persica, 182–83
Prunus persica var. *nucipersica*, 182–83
Psidium guajava, 150–51
pumpkins, 208–11
Punica granatum, 196–97
pyrethrins, 67
pyrethroids, 68
Pyrus communis, 184–85
Pyrus pyrifolia, 184–85

quinces, 200–201

radicchio, 163
radishes, 202–3
rain barrels, 54
raised beds, 29
Raphanus sativus, 202–3
raspberries, 114–15
Rheum rhabarbarum, 204–5
rhubarb, 204–5
root systems, 21
rotenone, 67
Rubus spp., 114–15
runner beans, 106–9
rust, 79
rutabagas, 224–25

scales, 70
school gardens, 18
seed exchanges, 40
Seed Savers Exchange, 26
seed saving, 39–41
seed sources, 26, 233
seed starting, 34–38
snap beans, 106–9
soil acidity, 12, 45
soil care, 42–48

soil depth, 21, 45–46
soil nutrients, 46–48
soil types, 12
Solanum melongena var. *esculentum*, 142–43
Solanum tuberosum, 198–99
Spinacea oleracea, 206–7
spinach, 206–7
square foot gardening, 28–29
squash, 208–11
Stevenson, Robert Louis, 13
strawberries, 212–13
summer squash, 208–11
sun exposure, 20, 22
Sunset Publishing Corporation, 27
     ing t*See also* cold-hardiness zones
sweet oranges, 132–35
sweet potatoes, 214–15
Swiss chard, 216–17

thyme, 218–19
Thymus vulgaris, 218–19
tilling soil, 43
tomatoes, 220–23
tools, 55–59
transplanting, 35–36, 39
tree grafting, 31
turnips, 224–25

University of California Fruit & Nut Research and Information Center, 27
USDA hardiness zones, 8–9, 12, 26–27

Vaccinium spp., 112–13
Valerianella locusta, 163
vertical planting, 29–30
verticillium wilt, 79
Vicia faba, 106–9
Vitis vinifera, 148–49

watering, 50–54
watermelons, 166–67
Waters, Alice, 13
weeding, 52
winter squash, 208–11

Zea mays, 136–39

MEET CLAIRE SPLAN

Claire Splan is a freelance writer and editor in Alameda, California. After buying her first house in 2002, she began taking horticulture classes and remaking the gardens at her home. She wrote about her experiences there and her growing interest in gardening and environmental issues at her garden blog, *An Alameda Garden* (www.alamedagarden.blogspot.com). A member of the Garden Writers Association, Claire has been published in the *San Francisco Chronicle*, *Rosebud*, and *Firsts* magazine and reviews gardening books for the *New York Journal of Books* (www.nyjournalofbooks.com). Claire has degrees from the University of Southern California and the University of San Francisco, and she has studied landscape horticulture at Merritt College.

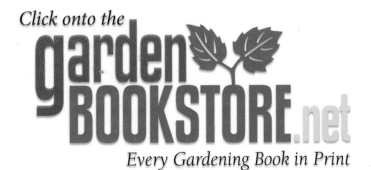